Memoir

by ROSARIO FERRÉ

Translated from the original Spanish
by
Suzanne Hintz and Benigno Trigo

Published by Bucknell University Press
Copublished by The Rowman & Littlefield Publishing Group, Inc.
4501 Forbes Boulevard, Suite 200, Lanham, Maryland 20706
www.rowman.com

Unit A, Whitacre Mews, 26-34 Stannary Street, London SE11 4AB

British Library Cataloguing in Publication Information Available

Library of Congress Cataloging-in-Publication Data Available

ISBN: 978-1-61148-662-9 (pbk. : alk. paper)
ISBN: 978-1-61148-663-6 (electronic)

♾™ The paper used in this publication meets the minimum requirements of American National Standard for Information Sciences—Permanence of Paper for Printed Library Materials, ANSI/NISO Z39.48-1992.

Printed in the United States of America

For my son Benigno,
traveling companion
across the landscape
of memory...

Contents

1
Prologue

5
The Word Became Flesh

79
How I Began to Write

111
Epilogue

113
Upon Entering the Academy

Prologue

Storytelling is a living consciousness:
knowing who you are, what is within you, and what you can do.
— SCHEHEREZADE —

The myrtle is a "flower that blooms"; after the rain, its perfume attracts ghosts. When I married and went to the capital city to live, Mother sent me some myrtle bushes from the patio of our house in La Alhambra. Our chauffeur Carmelo Bocachica brought them to me planted in Yaucono coffee cans. Those myrtle bushes were originally from the garden in Guanajibo and Mother had transplanted them to her garden in Ponce when she married and moved there to live. Mother told me that I should plant the bushes under my balcony so that I could enjoy their perfume at night, especially after it rained.

From childhood I realized that Mother did not like public life. The 1930s and 1940s were extremely difficult years, the dreadful decades of Puerto Rican history. Father soon became convinced that only through political action would he be able to help other Puerto Ricans. Nevertheless, for Mother politics were always "tales of sound and fury." She used to make fun of the statues of our founding fathers, facing a future so unhygienic as having one's head eternally shat upon by birds. When town leaders came to the Alhambra house heavy with presents like laying chickens with shiny feathers, baskets full of Nebo oranges, bananas or big pineapples, or when they sent ice boxes stuffed with red snappers, dog snappers and hogfish, Mother would thank them with a sad smile whose meaning only I understood. Those fruits of the land and the sea that they brought to her husband meant only one thing to her: one day Father would no longer belong to her. She would have to share him with everyone. And what was worse, she would stop belonging to her own self. She would lose her personal space forever, her right to silence and to walk on the sunny side of the street without being pointed out or recognized by anyone. What happened to her was what the members of certain tribes believe happens when someone captures their image. Their spirit no longer swims free and anonymous in the powerful current of universal energy. The spirit becomes part of history and its cultural patrimony.

Mother became gravely ill shortly after Father's successful run for governor of the Island in 1968. She understood that the end of her life was near. She did not want an elaborate funeral with public rites traditionally given to a leader's wife. She asked that her funeral be the simplest possible and that no one send flowers. She asked Father to make an announcement in the newspaper to that effect so that people would donate money anonymously to charitable causes. She has no pantheon with a roof. Scoured by the rain, sun, and wind, her simple tomb in the capital's cemetery today honors her preferences. Her tomb does not have a cross, bust, figure of a crying angel, nor a bleeding sacred heart that interrupts the white sobriety of its lines. It is for that reason that I dedicate this memoir to her.

The Word Became Flesh

I suppose that the literary vein comes to me from my mother's side. My maternal grandmother had a literary imagination that was out of control, as one can see by the names she gave to some of her daughters: Fredeswinda, Wagnerian valkyrie; Olga Acté, Russian czarina; Zorhaida, Cervantine heroine from his *Novelas Ejemplares*. I adored my eight maternal aunts. Aunt Haydée (Yiyi) and Aunt Olga were poets. They recited poetry during our Christmas dinners at the Guanajibo house, outside the city of Mayagüez. Yiyi had a natural talent for poetry. She was known for her poetry since her high school years in San Germán. There she won the beautifully provincial title of Princess of Poetry during a literary contest recital at the Mayagüez Athaneum. Later she earned recognition from the intellectual community when she earned her bachelor's degree at Río Piedras, where she met the Spanish poet Juan Ramón Jiménez. She published a beautiful book, entitled *Poesía*, with his support. My aunt was married to a Republican from the Spanish Civil War who had arrived in Puerto Rico as a refugee. My uncle was a gastroenterologist. He had in his office one of the first colonoscopes on the Island, and he taught at the University of Puerto Rico (UPR). Aunt Yiyi married him; and the Nightingale, as she was known, put aside her poetry. Aunt Olga, who also had poetic talent, married a brilliant botanist, an expert in phytopathology. She shut herself up in Cerro Las Mesas to write postmodern poetry, a style that fit her sweet and innocent personality well.

Rosario Ferré in the Colegio de Varones

From the time I was little, I wanted to be just like them, to be able to write and recite beautiful poetry but not to remain anonymous. I wanted to make writing my profession. My aunts spoke of a woman's world and they tried to interpret it. It was a way to look at the world that allowed them both to be useful and to transcend life, thanks to its spiritual values. My aunts' work was behind the scenes, eternal Penelopes who devotedly followed their husbands' orders.

When I was six years old, my parents enrolled me in the Colegio de Varones in Ponce, an elementary school that was mixed boys and girls until the fourth grade. I was completely happy there and never felt that anyone discriminated against me for being left-handed and female. The Marianist fathers were American and had an advanced educational philosophy for their time. But I experienced discrimination later, when I changed elementary schools. When I began fifth grade, my parents moved me to the Colegio del Sagrado Corazón, an institution still set deep in the Middle Ages. At that time Sagrado Corazón was an elitist institution charged with educating young girls from the upper class. Thus, all the students in the school were white and wrote with their right hands. Everyone knew that left-handers went to hell! Today it's completely different. Sagrado Corazón in Ponce closed some years later. It returned as an institution completely dedicated to social causes, and it did a world of good.

During summer vacation of 1954, I enrolled in the José H. Perry Secretarial School in Ponce. There I studied typing and learned to typewrite. I also tried to learn shorthand, but that proved to be too difficult. Only secretaries took shorthand and afterwards only they could understand what they had written. Men never learned shorthand. Shorthand was something that went with polished nails and women's needlework. When I understood this, I realized that I would never become a secretary.

The Ramírez de Arrellano family lived in Mayagüez and was very conservative. Even though they were rich, they lived frugally. Mother, Lorencita, was the oldest. She always dressed with great simplicity but in very good taste. Father's family, "the Ferrés," was middle class. They lived in great simplicity in a house on León Street in Ponce. They struggled to save so that they could send their four sons to study in universities outside Puerto Rico. My paternal grandfather, Papá Toño, was focused on forming a business in which all his sons could participate. For that very reason he never considered the option of sending them to study at the University of Puerto Rico. He wanted his sons to study engineering and business administration in order to create a family business. He achieved his goal. On the other hand, his daughters Rosario and Isolina were not supposed to study. Their destiny was to marry well and have a family. Saro studied through her second year of college, and Isolina only went to college when she was older. She earned her master's in sociology at Fordham University. By contrast, mother and her brothers and sisters all went to college. They studied in Europe and the United States. My uncle Alfredo paid for their education.

My mother was the oldest of ten children. She was born in San Germán in 1902. She attended elementary school at Imaculada Concepción in San Germán and later went to boarding school at Sagrado Corazón in Santurce. She studied there with her sister Freddy. Because they went away to boarding school together, they were always very close. Mother graduated from Sagrado Corazón in 1922. I still have

Lorencita Ramírez de Arellano (seated in the first row) next to her classmates the day of her graduation from eighth grade from the Sagrado Corazón School in Santurce

the gold cross for her graduation and a photograph of her sitting with her fellow students and the many prizes she won that day. At the time, Sagrado Corazón was located where the University of the Sagrado Corazón is located today, on one of the Monteflores hills, a neighborhood outside the capital.[1] Mother had an extraordinary intelligence and strong personality that helped her accomplish what she set out to do. She was beautiful and knew how to take advantage of her small height (five feet even) when she flirted with the opposite sex. I have a picture of her graduation from the University of Puerto Rico in which she wears a curl on her forehead, indicating she is single.

Mother majored in literature and education at the University of Puerto Rico and received her bachelor's degree in these fields. I inherited from her one of her textbooks, annotated in her own handwriting. It was a copy of the *Libro de Buen Amor*, written by the Arcipreste de Hita. She made me love Hispanic literature. After graduating from the University of Puerto Rico, Mother earned her master's degree in history

Lorencita Ramírez de Arellano
on her graduation from the
University of Puerto Rico

Lorencita Ramírez de Arellano at her graduation
from eighth grade at the Inmaculada Concepción
School of San Germán

Lorencita Ramírez de Arellano
on the day of her graduation from
the University of Puerto Rico

at Columbia University in New York. She went there to study with her friend Rosa Navarro. Of all the brothers and sisters, she was the one closest to having an intellectual career, even though two sisters, Dora and Haydée, did postgraduate work. Dora studied at Goucher College in Washington, D.C. and spent a period of time in Berlin in the time of Hitler. Haydée studied at The Catholic University of America in Washington, D.C. and later studied in Germany too.

For many years I considered Mother a typical woman of her generation. However, when I learned that she had gone to Santurce to study when she was 15, that she remained there for eight years until she graduated from the University of Puerto Rico in 1926, it was then I realized that she was an extraordinary woman. Her persistence was a sign of my grandparents' progressive determination to educate their eight daughters just like they educated their two sons. The eight years in Santurce also demonstrated that my mother was very brave to have dared to go to live in San Juan at such a young age, far from her family.

In the 1926 University of Puerto Rico yearbook, *El Athenea*, fellow students commented that she "loved teaching with real delight" and that "she will be the glory of Puerto Rican teachers." She was a Spanish teacher for three years, first at the Mayagüez high school, and later at the Guayama high school. She used to travel there weekly in her parents' Packard and stay with one of her aunts.

In 1927 she traveled to New York and visited Washington, D.C. She stayed at the home of her aunt María Luisa Barbot d'Haut Clair, a relative of her father's. Aunt María Luisa deserves special mention for being quite a personality. She was my grandfather's aunt, and her maiden name was Rosell. She had two sisters that had already died when I met her: Margarita and Pepita Rosell. Both sisters lived in Mayagüez. When Aunt María Luisa arrived in Guanajibo, my grandfather had already died. She became a lady's companion to my grandmother. Since she did not pay any rent to stay in the house, she mended my grandmother's clothing and crocheted doilies and small tablecloths for the furniture in exchange for her room and board. She was already in her seventies, yet she had returned to the Island with the dream of establishing a revolutionary dairy farm where the cows would be milked mechanically while they listened to music. Aunt María Luisa believed that listening to music would stimulate their milk production. She was, without doubt, ahead of her time. She bought a farm with her savings and went to live in the country far away in Maricao. She lived there alone, without furniture, and slept on the floor on a mattress. She never was able to realize her dream of starting a dairy farm. When she met the peasants who lived in the area, she realized they did not have access to a doctor. Since she had been a nurse in Washington, D.C., she dedicated herself to their care. Finally Aunt María Luisa gave up her dream of a dairy farm and became a kind of Florence Nightingale who made house calls, black bag in hand.

Mother rejected various suitors during the time she lived in San Juan, as she was in no hurry to get married. She met Father, Luis Alberto Ferré, at a dance at the Casino de Puerto Rico in San Juan. Later they saw each other again at a party in Ponce. My father invited her to dance with him. They were dancing together when Fernando Torréns tried to cut in. Torréns told Father that he was Lorencita's fiancé. Father told him that she had agreed to dance with him and why did Torréns not let her choose. Mother decided to dance with

*Lorencita Ramírez de Arellano
with Luis A. Ferré Aguayo*

*Wedding portrait of Lorencita Ramírez de Arellano
and Luis A. Ferré Aguayo*

Father and right then and there she returned Torréns's engagement ring. Father later used to tease her and say that she had thrown the ring on the floor because she was tired of Torréns. She danced all night with Father.

It was 1930 and Father was convalescing in the Damas de Ponce Hospital after an operation for appendicitis. He received a package with a copy of the novel *Green Mansions* by William Henry Hudson. The envelope did not have a return address. He enjoyed the novel, but it wasn't until he finished the book that my mother confessed that she had sent him the gift. That book was father's key to the enchanted forest of Guanajibo. Shortly thereafter they were engaged. Mother and Father married in 1931 at the Church of the Candelaria, now the cathedral of Mayagüez. They held the wedding reception in the Ramírez de Arellano house in Guanajibo. Mother was 29 and Father was 26. They spent their honeymoon in the Baños de Coamo, but I was not conceived there.

When I was little, I visited the Baños de Coamo often. I remember the baths of sulfuric water, the colonial style dining room with its

*Lorencita Ramírez de Arellano after her wedding dressed as a bride
in the first house in La Alhambra, 1931*

chairs upholstered in leather and adorned with bronze nails with lion heads, and the delicious water bread they served. I remember the ceiling fans, the first that I had ever seen. We did not use ceiling fans in Ponce. I remember the mosquito netting that hung from a wire frame above the pillow. The buildings were painted green and orange. The main building had a cement stairway with a double fan handrail. The check-in desk was there, and on the left was a hallway with blinds that opened to the rooms. The only bathroom was at the end of that hallway. There was an illegal casino, very popular with the residents of Ponce. When the police raided the place, the chief of police called the owner, don Pepín Targa, so that the visitors remained in their rooms. When the police arrived, there was no one there. I remember the bar at the top of an enormous saman tree that grew in the patio. Visitors reached it by climbing a ladder that was similar to the one in Tarzan's (Johnny Weissmuller's) tree house. Young people back then, "Mother and Father's friends," sometimes went up the saman for a drink, which was dangerous because they sometimes staggered when coming down the ladder.

The owners of the Coamo Baths were the Targa family, Pepín Targa's parents. Pepín Targa married Aileen Roig, Adalberto Roig's daughter. Uncle Adal had been Father's best friend and roommate at MIT. It was because of him that Aunt Saro (Rosario) met Adalberto, who became her husband. They had three children—Adalberto Jr., Aileen and Antonio. The alliance with the Roig family was without doubt convenient for the Ferré family and for Ponce Cement, a company that they would start in 1942.

Mother and Father's wedding added luster, money, and social position to my father's life. But she found herself trapped in an environment that was very different from her own. Having graduated from the University of Puerto Rico, her friends were different from Father's friends in Ponce. Her best friend, Rosa Navarro, was a professor of Natural Science at UPR for many years. Rosa was Mexican and married to Thomas Haydon, father to Tommy Haydon. Other friends

Carlos, Joe, don Antonio, Luis, and Hermán Ferré

*Antonio Luis, Luis A. Ferré, and don Antonio in front of the
Ponce Cement Factory*

of hers—Margot Arce, Cesáreo Rosa Nieves, Emilio Belaval, Vicente
Géigel Polanco—also were university professors. Father's friends were
from the San Juan middle class, ordinary people who lived the lifestyle
of the "roaring twenties."

When Aunt Saro married into the Roig family, members of the
sugar aristocracy of the Island, she connected the Ferré family with the
upper class of landowners. When they started Ponce Cement in 1942,
the Roig family invested a considerable amount of money, exactly half
of the initial capital. Years later, when one of my uncles began to invest
recklessly, the Roig family decided to get out of the company. They
sold their shares to the Ferré brothers and invested their capital in
Feldsmeer, a sugar mill located in Vero Beach, Florida.

Antonio Ferré Bacallao   *Mary Aguayo Casals*

PATERNAL GRANDPARENTS

Antonio Ferré Bacallao was born in 1877 in Havana, Cuba, in the barrio Güira de Melena. He died in 1959 in Ponce. They buried him in the Catholic cemetery in Ponce in the family pantheon next to my grandmother Mary Aguayo and his sons Carlos and Hermán Ferré. My grandfather moved to Puerto Rico in 1896, two years before the North American invasion of the Island. First he lived in San Juan, where he worked in the Abarca workshops. He was a mechanic by profession. It was much later, after the North Americans arrived on the Island, that he studied engineering by correspondence. Correspondence courses were not possible under the former Spanish regime. He moved to Ponce to work with one of his uncles, Luis Bacallao. There he met Mary Aguayo Casals. Grandfather Antonio and Grandmother Mary Aguayo had six children: Joe, Luis, Saro, Hermán, Carlos, and Isolina. Father, Luis Alberto, was born at 22 Aurora Street in 1904. He graduated from MIT in 1922.

My grandfather was the son of Maurice Ferré Perotín, an engineer and son of a French citizen, Louis Ferré Laforet. Ferré Laforet had immigrated to Cuba around 1840. Louis was originally from Deux Sèvres, a small village in the northeastern French province of Mèlle. He arrived in Cuba and was an agent of the French company Five Lille, a company that sold grinders and evaporators to sugar engineers. He married Marie Pauline Perotín in Mèlle. Their marriage license is among Father's papers at the Luis A. Ferré Foundation. Louis went to

Rosario Ferré with her father in front of the house at 22 Aurora Street in Ponce

Cuba to live. There he had a son, Maurice, with a Cuban woman. Later he returned to France with his son. There he learned that his attorney had robbed him of his life's savings, and he killed himself. His son enrolled in the École des Ponts et Chausées in Paris, where his uncle Luis Bacallao studied. Almost all the engineers that came to Panamá with Eiffel to build the Canal studied at the École.

Maurice was in Panama with Ferdinand de Lesseps when the French company went broke. Maurice returned to Cuba rather than return to France. There he married Rosario Bacallao and fathered two children, my grandfather Antonio and Isolina Ferré Bacallao. Maurice died in Cuba in 1894. He contracted pneumonia while installing a cold-storage plant in Havana. His wife had already died, and his son Antonio went to Matanzas to live with his grandmother doña Andrea Sánchez Bacallao. His cousins, Alberto and Horencio Nodarce Bacallao, were military officers under General Maceo and were in the Cuban jungle fighting for independence. Antonio's relatives feared for his safety and encouraged him to immigrate to Puerto Rico. Antonio left on a sail-boat. He arrived in San Juan with a revolutionary's machete wrapped in leather in his suitcase and six pesos in his pocket. The year was 1896, and he was nineteen.

My grandfather Antonio left behind a short biography that says:

I was born June 9, 1877, in Havana, on the island of Cuba.
I studied at the school of San Vicente, with the Paulist brothers,
and at Matanzas High School. After finishing school, I worked
for a year in an asphalt mine under the supervision of my uncle,
Luis Bacallao, who was an engineer. During the next two years
I was an apprentice mechanic. The first year I worked eleven
hours a day without pay. The second year I worked nine hours a
day for ten cents a day at the foundry and at the Fénix workshop in Matanzas. I continued working as the third engineer
at the Central Carmen, which belonged to Crespo. I was there
when General Maceo invaded, during the harvest at the time
of the revolution for Cuban Independence. That was when
my relatives decided to send me to Puerto Rico to be with my
uncle, Luis Bacallao, who was a mechanical engineer for the
plantations owned by the Gayá and Serrallés family. In May 1896
I began to work under my uncle's supervision as his assistant on
various mechanical projects around the island.

Two years into my stay in Puerto Rico, occupying forces
arrived. Spanish rule changed to American rule. At that time
I met my future wife, Mary Aguayo, may she rest in peace. Also
at that time, I took advantage of the fact that Serrallés needed
an engineer for the Puerto Rico sugar mill in Santo Domingo.
They hired me and sent me there for a little over a year. When I
returned to Puerto Rico from Santo Domingo in 1901, I married
Mary Aguayo and we had six children—two girls and four boys:
José, Luis, Carlos and Hermán, Rosario and Isolina. I gave them
all an education and prepared them for life. I consider that to be
my greatest accomplishment for the benefit of Puerto Rico and
of my own family.

Over time I assembled many sugar mills in Puerto Rico
and different kinds of machines. I founded Porto Rico Iron
Works, Inc., and I ran the business all by myself while my sons
completed their engineering degrees in the United States.
When they returned to Puerto Rico, they became my right
hand men and we grew and improved the business. With their
initiative and my assistance and cooperation, we started the
Ponce Cement Corporation. From there on you all know my
work and way of life.

Aunt Isolina, 1974

There is also my great aunt, the sister of my grandfather Antonio, whose name was Isolina. My own aunt was named after her. Isolina was younger than my grandfather. She showed she had an independent spirit when she was young. One day she ran away from home and became a nun. She became Mother Superior of the Sagrado Corazón in Marianao, where the daughters of wealthy Cubans were educated. She left Cuba in 1961 after Fidel Castro's revolution. She arrived in Puerto Rico, where she lived in the convent of the Apostolado of the Sagrado Corazón in the town of Aguirre. The family helped build the convent, where she taught poor children from the barrio el Coquí. She died at the age of 96 in 1975, her mind sharp as a tack.

The Luis A. Ferré Foundation has a letter Isolina wrote to my great great uncle Luis Bacallao and to my grandfather, who were in Puerto Rico at that time. In the letter she informs them of her decision to enter a convent in Havana as if it were a *fait accompli*. The letter is a declaration of independence by a seventeen-year-old. Isolina's parents were dead. Her uncle Luis Bacallao had left for Puerto Rico fleeing the revolution, taking his nephew Antonio with him. Isolina remained in Cuba living practically alone in her parents' home. The circumstances made it easy for her to escape and enter the convent. Probably my aunt suffered the consequences of the bloody war that waged all around her. These were the terrible days of General Valeriano Weyler. For her the convent could have been a place of refuge and security.

Havana, December 7, 1896
Don Luis Bacallao
Puerto Rico

Dear Uncle:

I hope you are well. I must tell you something that perhaps may surprise you. However, you cannot but give your approval if you give it some thought.

On the 27th of last month I joined a religious community in Havana that dedicates itself to education. I am very happy because I achieved my goal of consecrating myself to Our Lord for the rest of my life. My complete happiness is with Him. If Our Lord had had a different calling for me, I believe you would not have opposed it after seeing that my future well-being was assured. So I believe you will not disapprove of my decision knowing how happy I am. I will never forget the blessings I have received from you and from your dear wife, whom I love like a mother. I will never be able to repay you for everything you have done for me. The one thing I will do is to pray to Our Lord for your happiness.

From your niece who loves you,
Isolina

Dear Brother:

The letter I sent Luis will tell you the decision I have made. I do not think you will be upset because you know that the religious life is my happiness. I pray that you continue in the future as you are now. You will become a good man. Obey Luis in all things, he loves you like a son. Help him in any way you can, he deserves as much. Follow his advice and you will keep him happy. I am well here. I cannot begin to tell you how well they look upon me.

Good-bye dear brother. Never forget your sister's advice. I commend you to Our Lord and ask him for your happiness.

Isolina

Mary Aguayo Casals
This photo was on Luis A. Ferré's dressing table for many years.

My grandmother Mary Aguayo was born on the island of St. Thomas in 1879 and died in Ponce in 1931. Her parents lived in Charlotte Amalie, the capital of St. Thomas. There they had a store where they sold liquor and other imported goods. My grandmother's mother died, and my great grandfather Félix Aguayo became blind. He emigrated with his daughters Mary and Pepita to Ponce. There they had a relative, Don Luis Casals, who was a rich tobacco merchant and had a lottery shop. Luis helped Félix get a license to sell lottery tickets. Don Luis Casals is a relative of Don Pablo Casals. Father always felt very proud of that fact.

Since Mary spoke English, she possibly taught her children the language, something that later helped them be admitted to universities in the United States. Father always spoke of the Aguayos as a family of educators. Carlos Aguayo was a teacher in Bayamón. He also said there was an Aguayo that served as mayor of San Juan and was buried in a crypt in the San José Church in Old San Juan. This is the same church where Don Juan Ponce de León is buried. As a matter of fact, this was confirmed during the restoration of that church.

It bothered Father that Ramírez de Arrellano was a surname that belonged to the Spanish nobility. He got in touch with a charlatan who studied genealogy. That individual, supposedly, found proof that the surname Aguayo del Rey was noble because its roots came from "Aguas paso yo por mi rey" (I do anything for my king). My mother teased my father about that and never paid a bit of attention to it. Once in 1956 when we traveled to Córdoba, Father made contact with the Count of Villaverde, who was said to be a relative of ours on the Aguayo side. Father called him, and the count came to the hotel where we were staying. He was dressed in dirty, rumpled clothes. The so-called count was a slovenly type who immediately asked Father for a loan. Since then the Count of Villaverde never spoke to us again.

Father and his three brothers studied in the United States. Father, Hermán, and Carlos graduated from MIT, and Joe graduated from Boston University. Father and his brothers studied engineering, and Joe studied business administration. The Ferré Aguayo family also lived at 13 León Street. The house was made of wood and was near the Market Square in downtown Ponce. It had a cement balcony with wooden balusters painted green. Later my grandfather substituted them for wrought iron balusters painted a silver color. The balcony's floor was made of gray marble tiles. The floors in the house were hard-

Antonio Ferré and Josefina (Pepita) Goenaga in their Alhambra house, 1956

wood. The back of the house had a patio that was made of cement. The ceiling was made of wood and had two round fans. The fans looked like tin hats on each side of the zinc roof. There was a large garden behind the house where my grandmother planted her roses and my grandfather had an arbor where he grew purple grapes. The entire Ferré family used to get together for lunch in this house every Palm Sunday. This was a traditional family celebration that my grandfather always held with his second wife, Josefina Goenaga de Ferré. I never knew my grandmother because she died in 1931 before I was born. She died of filariasis, a little understood disease that at that time was not curable.

Lorencita Ramíez de Arellano, Luis A. Ferré, and Luis Antonio Ferré
in front of Porto Rico Iron Works (ca. 1935)

The children also got together in the house on León Street to celebrate birthdays every year. Pepita, the name my step grandmother used, was a baker. The house was always filled with desserts everywhere.

My grandfather had a foundry, Porto Rico Iron Works, where he made iron crushers and cast iron wheels for the Puerto Rican sugar mills. The experience that he had gained in Cuba with his uncle Luis Bacallao served him well. He knew exactly how to build the machines he had repaired so many times as a mechanic for the Cuban mills. Many of the parts for the Puerto Rican sugar mills formerly had been made in Scotland and later in the United States. There was a market for these parts in Puerto Rico, which served my grandfather well. Later, during the sugar crisis, Porto Rico Iron Works began to decline. My father and his brothers, who had already joined the foundry, realized that they needed other alternatives to strengthen the family business. In 1941 they started to think about a cement plant, despite the challenging global political situation. They needed sophisticated equipment: a clinker mill—a machine that produces the raw material in cement—something that they had never built in their foundry. They purchased the mill in Pittsburgh and twice shipped it to Puerto Rico. Each time, German submarines sunk the ships. In the end, my father and his brothers had to come up with a way to make a clinker mill from scratch in the Porto Rico Iron Works.

By 1940 my father was the head of the family even though he was not the oldest son. He made all the important decisions. He was spontaneous, a natural leader, who helped everything turn out well even in difficult situations. Once when he was driving at night on a road in the interior of the Island, two men swinging their machetes at one another were caught in the headlights. Disregarding my mother's screams, Father got out of the car and successfully separated them. Later some neighbors arrived to help him.

I was very happy when my grandfather moved to a new cement house that his sons built for him in 1955, across the street from our Alhambra house. I got along with my grandfather and every now and then we went for a ride to his country house in Adjuntas. He was very loving with me. In Adjuntas, he would take me to the strawberry patch to eat strawberries as we picked them. He was the first to teach me about the marvelous fragrance of the gardenia flower. When I turned eight years old, he gave me a diary in which I didn't write very often.

Rosario Ferré in the Adjuntas countryside

However, I do have a description of a time spent with him in the house on León Street on the evening of January 5, 1947. I wrote:

> I spent the Eve of Three Kings Day at my grandfather's house, and we played canasta until 1:00 in the morning. He had a bugle and toy cap gun that made a lot of noise. My grandfather had his three dogs next to him. Each time the largest of the three began to howl and bark, afraid of the noise on the street, he would blow the bugle and shoot the cap pistol. He wanted the dogs to get used to the noise. After a while we finished playing canasta and went outside to the street to take a walk. It was a marvelous scene.
>
> The sidewalks were filled with people strolling, visiting many little stores that had been set up at the last minute, selling string toys, little ducks, toads, little chickens, darts, kites, whistles, maracas, and many more things. They were cheap toys, almost all made of string, things that country people could afford to buy. I had never seen this before because my parents and grandparents always gave my brother and me toys purchased in stores like El Cometa and González Padín: dolls, skates, bicycles, lead soldiers. Yet our house in La Alhambra was missing the joy that spread through León Street on the Eve of Three Kings Day.

My father's brothers were very close. That bond contributed without doubt to the success of the family business. My grandfather designed a flag with a logo of four small cast iron wheels within a larger one. The logo carried the maxim "There is strength in unity." The cast iron wheel is one of the most important parts of a sugar mill. And it made sense that grandfather would think of it as a logo for the family business. This flag was flown in front of the business's offices. Father was the most handsome of all the brothers, and he had a strong personality. He won people over easily because of his empathy and intelligence. In the family business he was the organizer and administrator. His older brother José was the impresario who put together the business deals. He had a tremendous ability to find money as if he pulled it out of his sleeve. He was feisty and happy, always ready to tell a joke. Many times his humor was a sign of his shrewdness and perspicacity in business. Hermán and Carlos, the youngest brothers, always lived in the shadow of the other two. They worked in the business but were not the leaders. Carlos had a fragile personality. He died rather young of a heart attack after electroshock therapy. His death saddened my father greatly because Carlos was his favorite brother. All the brothers were alike: they were very generous, and they all supported their individual causes. Anonymously they helped many people.

The story of my aunt Isolina, Sister Thomas Marie, member of The Missionary Servants Of The Most Blessed Trinity, is too long and

Sister Isolina Ferré Aguayo

Cardinal Spellman, Sister Isolina Ferré, and family in the home of Mr. Antonio Ferré celebrating the founding of the Universidad Católica of Ponce, to which the Ferré family donated the land, 1959

complex to tell here. She wrote her own autobiography, *Puentes desde el centro*, that El Nuevo Día Press will publish. I do, however, want to document in this memoir that she was an extraordinary person who dedicated her life to working for the poor in Brooklyn, the Bronx, and in La Playa, a barrio of Ponce. Along with my grandfather she was the family member I loved the most.

After Carlos's death the solidarity of the family began to crack. José had made some very lucrative business deals in the cement industry in Florida. He asked to go his own way. José became the administrator of the cement business there, Maule Industries, and the other brothers remained with the Puerto Rico business. Business went well in the beginning, but the oil crisis of the seventies caused an untenable situation. Maule went bankrupt.

From 1945 to 1960 my childhood and adolescence in the Alhambra house were happy. My aunts and uncles all lived in houses near ours.

Front row: Rosaloren Trigo, Luis Trigo, and Benigno Trigo; Back row: Memé Ferré,
Luis A. Ferré, and Rosario Ferré at La Fortaleza

My grandfather lived across the street. This gave me a sense of familial stability.

In 1968 Father won the election and became Governor of Puerto Rico until 1972. It was a marvelous experience. We had all worked hard on the political campaign of a brand new Partido Nuevo Progresista. Father had not expected to win. He had run three times for governor and had lost every time. He had to write his acceptance speech quickly on an empty envelope at two o'clock in the morning in the Party offices at Parada 22. From the top of the building everyone could hear the cars honking and people shouting and celebrating in the streets below; we were all possessed by the spirit of the moment.

Father, my brother, and I were convinced that we were living the beginning of a new era for Puerto Rico. The country was changing, and Father helped to bring a breath of fresh air to the Island. People were tired of the long rule of the Partido Popular Democrático and also

Grandchildren of Luis A. Ferré with Lorencita Ramírez de Arellano in La Fortaleza

of their Republican opposition, led by Miguel Ángel García Méndez, always the same party bosses.

The issue of the Island's political status was only superficially in my thoughts at that time. In Ponce people did not focus on what happened in Puerto Rican, European, or North American culture. People focused on sports, on the basketball star Pachín Vicéns, even though Albizu Campos was from Ponce. When I helped Father's campaign, it was not because I believed in statehood. It was because I wanted to help him win the election.

Father's rise to the governorship affected the family in many ways. On the night of Father's victory, Mother was in Ponce, a prisoner of an oxygen tent used to treat her heart condition. Father called her immediately to give her the news. Even though she was not enthusiastic about his political cause, her support for my father was always unconditional. She moved to La Fortaleza and called her childhood friend

Rosa Navarro to come help her. Rosa served as her anonymous executive secretary for four years. Rosa helped Mother write hundreds of letters that kept her in contact with the Puerto Rican people. This was very important for my father's public image.

Mother's death in 1971 left my father devastated. As always happens, one knows that the person who suffers from a serious illness can die at any moment. But one is never prepared for the blow when it hits. I was in my house on Marbella, seated at my desk paying bills, when I felt a terrible disturbance. I felt an irrepressible urge to visit Mother. I used to visit her three or four times a week but that day I ran to get into the car. I drove like a crazy person to La Fortaleza, running several traffic lights. When I arrived, there was a commotion in the private apartments. I found Federico Torres Campos standing in front of the door to the bedroom, like a black vulture, stopping everyone from coming in. When I entered I saw Father giving artificial respiration to Mother. While trying to revive her, he told her, "Don't worry, Cita. I'm here. Nothing's going to happen to you."

When the inevitable was accepted by all the doctors and they declared Mother dead, Father went alone to another room at the back of the apartment to cry. I remained with my mother while Miss Rita Guzmán, mother's nurse, began the first rites to prepare the body. In that absolute silence I spoke to her in my heart, and I asked her forgiveness for all the faults that I had committed against her. To be with her during those moments was a great consolation for me.

Father lost the 1972 election despite all of the social good his government did during his four years in office. He surrounded himself with people who not good enough to govern cleanly, and the scandals that took place hurt his image. Father was very naïve even with his dazzling intelligence. And he was a bad judge of character. Shortly after the victory my brother and I realized this but Father did not allow anyone from the family to help him. He appointed unscrupulous politicians who took advantage of him. Given the chance, they would have stolen the nails from the Holy Cross.

The family business suffered during the four years my father served as governor. Before becoming governor, Father had to give up his position as chief executive officer of the family business. Three of the four factories that the family had bought from the government at the beginning of the 1950s—Puerto Rico Clay, Puerto Rico Paper and

Rosario Ferré with her brother Antonio Luis Ferré

Pulp, and Puerto Rico Glass—were managed by my uncles and were on the verge of bankruptcy. The only ones doing well were the Cement Plants, the one in Ponce and the other in San Juan. Both were run by my brother Antonio Luis Ferré. Thanks to him the family was able to overcome the crisis in Puerto Rico. Maule in Florida, run by my uncle Joe, was gone with the wind.

MATERNAL GRANDPARENTS

Alfredo Ramírez de Arellano, Papipo, was born in 1883 on the Manantiales de Guánica estate. His mother, Lorencita Rosell, died of typhus when she was 18 years old. His father, Ubaldino Ramírez de Arellano, married again. Lorencita was the daughter of a colonel in the Spanish army whose portrait hung in the dining room of the Guanajibo house. Alfredo was raised by his paternal uncle Quintín Ramírez de Arellano. My grandfather called him Papatío. The new wife of Ubaldino (senior) was Mary Quiñones, mother of Uncle Ubaldino, Uncle Gustavo, and Aunt Haydee. They were all from San Germán. Lorencita left some jewels that I chanced to see: a gold and diamond ring in the form of a slanted cross, an onion watch with a pearl bird enameled on top, and some ruby earrings in the form of small scarabs. All of it was lost. Papipo did not go to the university. He was privately tutored. Everything he knew about the sugar industry he learned from experience, growing up in the fields.

When his father died, the Manantiales estate passed into the hands of his half brothers. The estate had been in the family for generations. When the half brothers found themselves in financial difficulties, they

Alfredo Ramírez de Arellano Rosell

*Alfredo Ramírez de Arellano with
Quintín Ramírez de Arellano (Papatío)*

Central Igualdad in Mayagüez

offered both the estate and the Guánica Sugar Mill to North Americans for less than its real value. My grandfather borrowed money from the bank and used the jewels he had inherited from his mother as collateral. With that money he was able to purchase the land from his half brothers. My grandfather had a document signed when his mother died stating that he had the right of first refusal on the property. In other words he had the first option to purchase the land at the same price offered to the North Americans. Later my grandfather purchased the Ana María Sugar Mill that belonged to the Valdés family. This business was enormously productive. He changed the name of the mill to Igualdad.

The Ramírez de Arellano family came from the village of Arellano, near the city of Estela in Old Castile. In the 1970s I traveled to Castile to find the family home. It had the family crest, three rivers of silver on a field of blue, chiseled above the entrance to the garden as well as a tower made of stone in one of the corners of the house. Supposedly the tower was built for a sentry during the war against the Moors. The family seat had its own chapel and was surrounded by a wall.

Intendant Ramírez, first Secretary of Housing in Puerto Rico during colonial times, was their descendent. One branch of the family

Alfredo Ramírez de Arellano
dressed as a boxer

Alfredo Ramírez de Arellano and
Josefa Bártoli (Pepé) in Guanajibo

went to live in Mexico, and another remained in San Juan. The latter was related to the ancestors of Mariíta Ramírez de Arellano de Vizcarrondo and to the architect Lorenzo Ramírez de Arellano, all of them distant relations of ours.

Grandfather Alfredo married Josefa Bártoli y Martínez. Her family was from Peñuelas and Cabo Rojo. Josefa's father, Estéfano or Etienne Bártoli, arrived in Puerto Rico in 1860. He was 24 years old and a native of Corsica from the rural Sisco peninsula. He married Monserrate Martínez, daughter of a landowner from the town of Peñuelas. I discovered Estéfano's story after a visit with the architect Enrique Vivoni, who was director of the School of Architecture at UPR. Enrique was in Corsica and did research on the houses of Puerto Rican Corsicans there. During his stay on Corsica he discovered some letters containing Estéfano's tragic story. I have a copy of those documents as well as his order of imprisonment.

Estéfano worked the land. He had a farm in Mata de Plátano, a barrio of Peñuelas. In 1888 he found himself in a very difficult economic situation. In order to pay his debts he sold eight hectares directly to

Josefa Bártoli in San Germán

Carlos Defendini Vivoni. There was no written agreement. Defendini Vivoni refused to pay Estéfano, who later had to declare bankruptcy. Estéfano was desperate, and he killed Defendini, Enrique Vivoni's great uncle. There is another version of what happened according to my cousin Fredita García Méndez. When Monserrate learned of Defendini's misdeed, she went looking for him on horseback. When she found him, she shot him four times. Later Estéfano confessed to the crime to prevent his wife from going to prison. The documents and the order for Estéfano's incarceration are stored in Ponce's city hall. Estéfano Bártoli served seven years in prison. No one really knows the truth of what happened, and the secret remained with the family.

Estéfano died in 1904. He is buried in the cemetery of the town of Yauco, in the pantheon of don Domingo Mariani.

Estéfano Bártoli had five children: Alfonsa, Estéfana, Josefa (my grandmother whom they called Pepé), María, Pompeyo, and a second son who died of epilepsy and whose name I do not remember. I visited the house where Uncle Pompeyo, Aunt Estéfana, and Aunt María lived together. None of them married. They lived in San Germán on the street that runs right through the town on the way from Mayagüez to Ponce. It had a small balcony with silver colored balusters in front and a beautiful rose bush. In the back there was a gallery of balconies that looked over the Santa Marta hills. Aunt María was tiny at only five feet tall. They called her Mariíta. She was a medium and claimed to be in contact with José de Diego and Luis Lloréns Torres. She had a blackboard on the kitchen wall where she wrote down poems that the two poets dictated to her.

Aunt Alfonsa married a Corsican, don Domingo Mariani, known as don Ton Ton. They were Nuni Mariani's grandparents. Nuni Mariani married Jaime Viqueira, father of my cousin Ileana Viqueira.

The Mariani family lived in Yauco in a beautiful house called Hacienda Rogliano. They even had a French tutor for the children. Don Ton Ton was a wealthy coffee grower. He had an estate in the higher elevations of Río Negro, along the highway to Peñuelas. One day I managed to visit the estate. It was raining cats and dogs. I remember the tahona, the enormous mill or wheel to grind coffee, a stone weighing several tons. It must have taken God and his Apostles to climb the hills of Río Negro with the wheel on muleback. The Hacienda was a mythical place for Mother. She had spent long periods of time there as a little girl. But the house lost its charm when don Andrés Grillasca, Ponce's mayor, bought it. They say that Luis Muñoz Marín joined his drinking buddies there for a good time. Don Ton Ton also owned Hacienda Albina in the valley of Lajas. It was a huge house with a lake and swans in the front yard. He also owned Hacienda Santa Rita at the entrance to the town of Guánica. It was there that my grandfather met my grandmother.

Don Ton Ton went bankrupt because of the coffee crisis at the beginning of the twentieth century when the market bottomed out after the North American occupation. When I was a little girl, Hacienda Rogliano and Albina had disappeared, but Santa Rita was

Alfredo and Josefa with two of their daughters—Lorencita and Fredeswinda

still standing. It is a house with a silver-colored balcony all the way around it, marble floors, and a fan stairway in the back. There are half a dozen stables at the back of the house, in an old building with an arched gallery.

My grandparents Alfredo and Josefa met in 1902. Perhaps because of her father's misfortune, Josefa had gone to live with Alfonsa, her older sister. According to family legend, Alfredo saw Josefa for the first time when he passed in front of their house riding horseback. She was sitting with a baby on her lap. He thought she was married, as they say. When he found out she was single, he asked Mariani for permission to court her. They married that same year and went to San Germán to live. My grandmother was 16 years old, and she began immediately to have children; she had ten in a row.

Mother and the other older sisters were born in San Germán. The family lived there only part of the year. When it stopped raining in December and the sugar cane began to ripen in the fields, they moved to Sambolín, an old country house on the outskirts of San Germán. Since the family had been absent for six months, they were well received by the servants and farm hands because their salaries would go up, especially if the harvest was good. By then the danger from hurricanes was over. The following months would bring little rain and a fresh breeze. "April rains will fill a barrel, but May rains will fill one horse," Grandfather Alfredo would say with a laugh. Mother and her brothers and sisters were completely happy in Sambolín, perhaps because they did not have to go to school. That gave them more time to ride horseback, travel in ox carts, and swim in the nearby river.

Lorencita Ramírez de Arellano (on the right) with her sister Fredeswinda

Lorencita Ramírez de Arellano (on the right) with her sister Fredeswinda

Lorencita Ramírez de Arellano and her brothers and sisters in San Germán

Lorencita Ramírez de Arellano with her brothers and sisters

Sambolín was very important to me. I managed to get myself photographed in front of it before they tore it down. It was the first place where my memory and my imagination came together in a single reality. I never went inside because the stairway and the rotted wood floors had become a danger to anyone who tried to climb them. But thanks to Mother's description, I knew it like the palm of my hand. It had wooden plank floors and a gabled zinc roof that turned into an orchestra during a heavy downpour. It also had a flying out-house facing the sugar cane fields. It allowed Grandfather Alfredo to

Young Lorencita

*Lorencita Ramírez de Arellano at the Reign of
the Dolls at the Mayagüez Casino*

*Lorencita Ramírez de Arellano with her brothers and sisters at the
Sambolín hacienda (ca. 1920)*

fertilize his sugar cane with the turds of his family. The house also had
a fan stairway, a provincial copy of the one from the castle of Fontaine-
bleu in France. It was a traditional country house with a warehouse
on the lower level. A balcony wrapped around the upper floor and the
house was surrounded by sugarcane. In front there was a batey, an open
space where the indians and the slaves were gathered together in ear-
lier times. Nearby, in a bamboo forest, there was a stream, and further
away there was a river where they took the children in covered oxcarts
to get bathed. Today the old country house has disappeared together

Rosario Ferré at the Sambolín hacienda (ca. 1945)

with the sugar cane fields that surrounded it. Even the road has fallen into disrepair because everybody now takes the highway between Mayagüez and San Germán. I treasure the photograph from Sambolín as a magic charm and as the only proof that reality and fiction are different. Sambolín is a complex place that signifies for me the fusion of memory and imagination, reality and fiction.

In 1923 my grandfather Alfredo's family moved to Mayagüez, where at first they lived on McKinley Street and later moved to the country house in Guanajibo that my grandfather purchased when the Bianchi

The Guanajibo house

family returned to Mallorca. From the balcony of Guanajibo, we could spy on the passage between Mona Island and Desecheo Island that seemed suspended on the horizon like an emerald. It was a beautiful blue sea that contrasted with the sea of sugar cane we saw from the balcony of Sambolín. If my mother's childhood had been connected to Sambolín and to its sea of sugar cane, the sea in Guanajibo opened her eyes to the future. Guanajibo represented the passage from adolescence to adulthood, the beginning of the period of travel, the discovery of the world. It was as if the Caribbean Sea expressed the family's desire to forget the painful source of wealth. The country house's ample verandas were not made of rustic wooden planks like the house in Sambolín. They were made of Puerto Rican polished cement tiles with blue, yellow, and green arabesques. We felt like dancing when we walked on them. Planters filled with ferns, myrtle, and Impatients circled the place. The plants multiplied almost magically without anyone taking care of them because there was so much rainfall daily. The eaves extended out like wide wings made from green tile all around the country house. One could almost say that the house was an excuse to justify the existence

Alfredo, Ángeles, Nino, Flor Ramírez de Arellano, and Franz Phillippi in front of the Guanajibo house

of that balcony. Mayagüez Bay surrounded it like a mirror of mercury, and at night the quiet sound of the waves came through the open windows like the very essence of a dream.

It was a large house with two floors, but everyone lived on the second floor. When friends and relatives visited the house, they climbed up to the second floor and did not need to go back down until they were ready to leave. For thirty-five years the family spent Christmas Eve in Guanajibo. At that time we were a clan of sixty plus people. But Guanajibo had room enough so that family members could spend that night in the house. We celebrated the occasion with a grand banquet similar to the one described by Ingmar Bergman in *Fanny and Alexander*, a film that profoundly affected me. The forty plus cousins got together to laugh and have a good time. Today we all remember the joy of those moments as something extraordinary.

When my grandmother Mamita Pepé died of cancer in 1964, it was as if the keystone of Guanajibo gave way. The family began to split up. Mamita Pepé had been the mortar of family solidarity. She was an extraordinary woman. From a very young age she dedicated herself to the care of her ten children. When they were grown and began to get sick and die from natural causes, she continued to take care of them with the same dedication as before. She would stand all night long by my mother's bedside, who was ill for eight years, saying prayers from

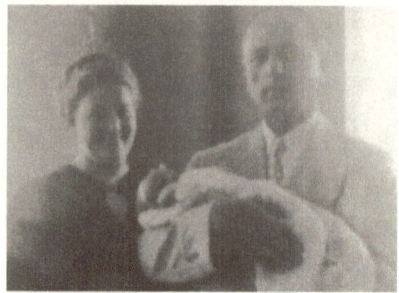

Pepita Goenaga and Alfredo Ramírez de Arellano with
Rosario Ferré in his arms on the day of her baptism

From left to right: Zorhaida, Ubaldino, Dora, Josefa, Alfredo, Lorencita, Flor, Fredeswinda,
Olga, Haydée, Alfredo, and Felicidad (seated on the floor) in the Guanajibo garden (ca. 1930)

many religions: Catholic, Christian Science, spiritist, and Rosicrucian. For me, her strength was an example of the courage of the Puerto Rican woman.

My maternal grandfather remained a country gentleman who did not trust city life. A relative of his had been an encomendero and had received an encomienda from the King of Spain. The family never spoke of that. The only time he traveled to Europe with the rest of the family was because Mamita Pepé forced him to go. Mamita Pepé felt that one trip was worth two university degrees. Then, my grandfather almost died from melancholy because he could not find sweet crabs in tomato sauce, rice with pigeon peas, or deep-fried plantains at the Cafe Procope in Paris.

I remember my grandfather clearly. He was a tall man with clear eyes, more than two meters tall. He was heavily built and very loving. I have a picture of him dressed in a white linen suit, holding me in his arms at my baptism. He was my godfather. I have three memories of Grandfather Alfredo: when he made his wedding ring dance on the dining room table, when he wound the grandfather clock in the living room, and when he invited me to look into his wardrobe. I do not know why he did this. Perhaps I was bored, and I was bothering him. He took out a switch-blade knife with a Mother of Pearl handle. Pushing a secret release button, he opened the shining blade in the darkness. Then he showed it to me and said, "I always carry it with me and if someone throws me off my horse, I'll cut his throat." I do not know why he said this to me, but it really surprised me that my grandfather, who was the sweetest man, had enemies that wanted to kill him.

The house in Guanajibo marked the moment of greatest prosperity for my grandfather thanks to the profits from sugar at the end of the First World War. Life in Guanajibo was very private, and the garden was the perfect expression of the desire of its inhabitants for anonymity. The family realized that it was a mythical garden. The garden expressed, much more than any other place I have known since, the right to personal happiness and to dream, the right to a space of one's own where one could identify with nature and also be transformed. With its illusion right out of Rousseau, with its exuberant tropical landscape far from reality, the garden declared the need to recover a lost innocence; it announced a world different from the "outside" where justice and beauty were not at odds with each other.

Front row: Alfredo Jr., Alfredo, Haydée, Josefa, Lorencita, Ileana, Fredeswinda, Fredita;
Back row: Dora, Zorhaida, Flor, Nino, Felicidad, and Olga on the balcony of the
Guanajibo house (ca. 1930)

The photos taken in that house are the proof of the existence of that improbable paradise, more so than any description. In the photos, Mother and her five sisters are dressed in organdy peeking out from behind the stone planters of the balcony and leaning over the dark waters of fountains like allegorical nymphs listening to the chords of Schubert's *Impromptu*. They all looked alike. They had the same long neck, Greek nose, and a strange way of walking as if gliding on water. The people of Mayagüez called my grandfather the Zeus of Guanajibo Abajo, father of the eight Ledas from Olympus. But the swans had their grotesque counterparts in the half dozen gaggling geese that grazed around the house. The ferocious geese attacked any unsuspecting stranger that inadvertently entered the garden, running after him, their orange maws wide open.

A wall more than twelve feet high surrounded the four acres of land and separated the house from the terrible reality of Puerto Rico at the time. In 1929 the average salary of a rural worker was $150 a year. Infant mortality due to uncinariasis, tuberculosis, and anemia was high. Murder and suicide among farmers were everyday occurrences. On the other hand, in the protected world behind the wall at Guanajibo, there was everything necessary for daily life: vegetables, fruit trees, cattle, chickens, ducks, pigs, and crab cages where the sweet water crabs fattened themselves eating corn. We even had stables.

The family had a house in Joyudas where we would go for day trips. We went there together and brought huge pans of chicken and rice, boiled green bananas, and lots of desserts like curdled cake, coconut and corn custards, and rice pudding. The forty cousins went to the beach there for twenty years. The beach at Joyudas was white, very different from Ponce where the sand was black, and far away, in front of us, we saw Ratones Island floating in the distance.

Family pastimes included walks under the hundred-year-old saman trees, tennis matches, a Spanish-language library that included the classic Latin American texts, swimming at the beach, sailing on the bay, and meals served by house staff who had always lived under the same roof as their masters. Just like the Finzi Continis, the family avoided leaving its garden for many years until world violence, sugar worker strikes, nationalist riots, and finally the ruin of the sugar industry forced them to come out.

The slogan for the inhabitants of the house was aesthetic sensibility, which they practiced as if it were the family ethos. That kind of sensibility had nothing to do with art. It was a discipline never put into words but implicit in their customs. It was in harmony with my grandparents' austerity. Even though the evening meals were carefully prepared, the serving bowls passed at the table were never filled to overflowing. Dinner guests from outside the compound often did not dare put food on their plates when they saw there were eight others waiting to be served.

I remember one family meal when my first husband, Benigno, was unexpectedly embarrassed when he was presented with a bowl of rice with pigeon peas. Benigno had come from a family of Spanish immigrants accustomed to sumptuously enjoying their stuffed pork shoulders and Serrano hams. The bowl of rice with pigeon peas seemed so small to him that he almost did not dare serve himself for fear of leaving the bowl empty. He thought that my grandmother was making fun of him when she scolded him for not having taken more. Benigno was convinced that the reason for that economy was that the family was stingy, a quality that he admired (being from the region of Extremadura in Spain), but that was unthinkable for him in the context of enjoying fine foods.

An architectural detail also contributed to Guanajibo's economic austerity: the skylights in the roof that gave light to the house. Besides saving electricity, the skylights gave the rooms a special atmosphere. There is something dreamlike in spaces lighted by vertical light. It is very different from light that comes from the street and enters through the windows. Vertical light does away with passing shadows, and what happens in those rooms is always for the best. There is no reason to fear what life might bring.

From 1923 to 1979 the Ramírez de Arrellano family lived in the house at Guanajibo. My grandfather Alfredo worked the land of his estate, and when he was elected Union Party member of the Chamber of Representatives, he traveled periodically to San Juan. He had a flagpole in the garden where he raised the Puerto Rican flag every day. When Luís Muñoz Marín's agrarian reform started, the government expropriated his land left and right and his business went down hill. The family spoke about Muñoz Marín as if he were an ogre, a henchman of Franklin D. Roosevelt, whom my grandfather always called "that stinking devil," because together they had come up with that taxation business. My grandfather died in 1946 from a heart attack. He had a prostate problem and they took him to Johns Hopkins to operate. During the operation his body did not assimilate the anesthesia, and the pain was so intense that he suffered a heart attack. He survived the attack, but from then on he suffered from heart problems and arteriosclerosis. He lost his mind in the end and died in the cabin in Cerro de Las Mesas that my grandparents built as a summer home. My grandmother and grandfather were buried in the Vivaldi cemetery on the outskirts of Mayagüez, in a pantheon that shelters many members of the family.

THE ALHAMBRA HOUSE

The houses we have lived in are special places that hold memories that remain after the owners disappear. Together, they form a mysterious geography and map who we were and who we never became. For that reason I have shared my memories of Guanajibo, Sambolín, and the house on León Street. But I have not yet made peace with the ghost of my mother. Perhaps I will do so by remembering the Alhambra house.

Father and Mother went to Ponce in 1931 to set up their house. First they lived for a few years on the outskirts of town in a very pretty house in La Alhambra. Father had fixed it up especially for the two of them for when they married. Uncle Joe owned the house, and Father rented it from him. There, on their wedding night, Father played Beethoven's *Appassionata* for Mother on the Bechstein grand piano, a wedding gift from Grandfather Alfredo.

La Alhambra was a neighborhood of partially run-down country houses at the edge of town, most of which were owned by the sugar cane bourgeoisie. The Cabasas, the Cortadas, and the Neumanns were some of the better-known families who began to have financial troubles in those days. All of our neighbors, however, insisted on living a life of uncontrolled fantasy. The forties and fifties were turbulent decades marked by the nationalist uprisings, the sugar cane strikes, and the Korean War. Things were coming to a head, but the Island bourgeoisie hid from reality in their hermetically sealed mansions.

The Alhambra's Club Deportivo was their traditional gathering place. The Club was surrounded by a beautiful wall of river stone, and an enormous sign hung over the front gate that read "if you are not a member, do not enter." An anonymous hand had been quick to deface the sign, scribbling in angry red letters, "if you are not a cheat, do not enter." The Club was next to a slum, and the boys from Machuelito had easy access to its grounds. Every so often they would take over the volleyball and basketball courts. The Portugués River bordered one side of the Club, with the shacks of La Milagrosa neighborhood piling up on its banks. There, one could find the infamous street vendors, lottery ticket hucksters, and swindlers from Guadalupe Street, commanded by the old Spanish Infantry barracks, recently transformed into the District court and county jail. The huge backyards of the homes from the Alhambra bordered the other side of the Club, and at night they became very dangerous due to their thick vegetation.

Children's Carnival at the Ponce Club Deportivo. Rosario Ferré, Queen of Music (ca. 1948)

We celebrated parties at the Sports Club in the 1920s and 1930s with exotic themes like the Court from a Thousand and One Nights, the Kingdom of Music, and the Kingdom of Dolls. Those parties were closer in spirit to the novels of Pierre Loti than to the social and economic reality of Ponce. The economic situation worsened the violence on the Island during the 1940s. Many people would leave their homes armed with weapons, in an effort to protect themselves from the unemployed wandering the streets. In those days the police rounded up people in search of a murderer known as Correa Cotto who had escaped from jail. They caught him, but only after he set fire to the cane field next to our house in La Alhambra.

The Second World War made matters worse, and the parties at the Club Deportivo were cancelled. They only celebrated the Children's Carnival, and in 1948 the directors chose me as the Queen of Music. My parents loved the idea. Adela Nones was in charge of the project. She was one of the ladies from La Alhambra and a friend of my mother's. She was portly and very kind. When she sang and danced, she was so entertaining that everyone forgot she was fat. She was very artistic. She had the ability to design stage sets, masks, and everything that had to do with the theatre. She created a giant lyre for my throne. It was covered completely with frost, something that went well with the frescos adorning the ceiling, painted by don Miguel Pou and depicting the Muses from Olympus.

Nothing remarkable would happen during the crowning ceremony of the king and queen. The new queen paraded on the arm of the king, followed by their court. They sat down on the throne, and the two previous queens carried the crown on a pillow and placed it on the head of the new queen. Adela had designed my dress and also those of my ladies in waiting. They were my best friends at the time—Neisa Deynes, Anadel Bravo, and Hania Lahongrais. They were dressed respectively as Chopin's *Nocturne*, Debussy's *Claire de Lune*, and Rimsky Korsakov's *Scheherezade*. Neisa's dress was of black tulle with a frosted star on her head. Anadel's was of blue tulle with a gigantic, frosted moon on her forehead. Hania's costume had lovely pants with pearls hanging from her waist to her feet and a top of silvered lamé. My dress was organdy, embroidered with musical notes of mother-of-pearl sequins. I wore a headpiece with the treble clef in rhinestones and other decorative stones. There was a kind of provincial ingenuity in all of this that had its charm. The Deportivo, designed by the Ponce architect Alfredo Wiechers in the thirties, was a very elegant building in its heyday, though by this time it had deteriorated a great deal. Water seeped through the roof, and the paint was chipping off the beautiful frescos by don Miguel Pou that decorated it. Guests on the dance floor could hear roosters crowing from the slum houses on the banks of the Portugués River that adjoined the club at the back of the property.

The coronation began at seven in the evening. The orchestra from Ponce's Escuela Libre de Música played. At my father's suggestion I walked to the chords of Chopin's *Concerto No. 2*. I felt very proud because I really believed that I was the queen of music, when the pageant was nothing more than an excuse to celebrate the music of the Polish genius.

When the economic crisis from the 1930s became more acute, my parents moved from the Alhambra house to Extensión Mariani, a middle class neighborhood in the center of the old city of Ponce.

*Lorencita Ramírez de Arellano with Rosario and Antonio Luis Ferré at the house on
General de la Torre Street in the Mariani extension of Ponce (1939)*

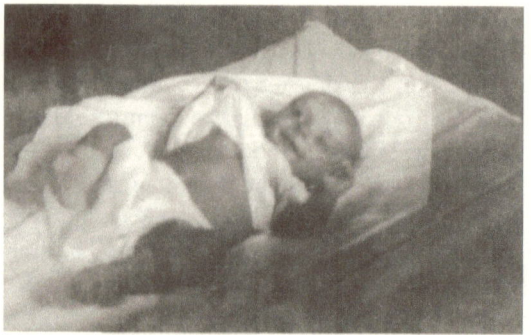

Baby Rosario Ferré at the Mariani house

They lived on Concordia Street, next to the Damas Hospital where my brother Antonio Luis was born in 1932. Later they lived on General de la Torre Street, where I was born in 1938.

In 1942 we moved back to La Alhambra at 2 Reina Mora Street. Father built the house with the first sacks from the recently built Ponce Cement plant. The factory was built with assistance from the federal government and it was planned so that it might serve its needs. It was also built just in time to provide the cement to build the dry dock in Ensenada, next to Fajardo. It was one of the largest dry docks in the world, with enough room for American battleships and submarines.

The new house, designed by Father, was a great promotion for the cement plant since it looked like it was built for eternity. The ad campaign was "Build with Ponce Cement: fire-, crack- and termite-proof."

Luis A. Ferré with Lorencita Ramírez de Arellano at the Alhambra house

Luis A. Ferré at the piano

The idea was that there were two advantages to building the house (the seat of the family) with Ponce cement. First, the family would be safe from natural disasters. Second, it would be safe from the social upheavals caused by the strikes of the sugar industry, such as the fires set in revenge to the cane fields and haciendas. The cement house made us feel secure. It identified us with modernity and progress. But more importantly it made us feel we no longer lived in Latin America and that we could escape from the natural disasters of the tropics. Living in a cement house was almost like living in the north, where there were no earthquakes, no white ants, no termites, and no hurricanes. Security, progress, modernity was the slogan of the cement plant in those years, heralding the mystique of the Partido Nuevo Progresista 20 years later.

We played the piano often in my house in La Alhambra. At night, you could hear the strains of Liszt, Grieg, and Schumann rising over the purple trinitaria that covered the walls. To these private concerts was added the reverence beyond any measure for classical music, considered by my parents to be the queen of the arts, for its power to

Luis A. Ferré and Lorencita Ramírez de Arellano at the Alhambra house

elevate the spirit to the sublime. My father used to play Beethoven's *Concerto No. 3.* That concerto was for me an introduction to absolute beauty, to the possibility of the soul's immortality. If that concerto existed, then we came from somewhere at birth and we were headed somewhere when we died.

The new house combined the California with the Criollo style. It had a red tile roof and two balconies. One of the balconies had huge arches that were reminiscent of the arches of the missions of New Mexico. The other balcony on the second floor had wrought iron balusters painted white in imitation of the architectural motifs of the houses in Ponce. The ceiling on the California balcony was very high.

From the beginning my mother painted it a bluish turquoise as if she wanted to bring the clear, blue, cloudless sky inside the house, that same sky that covers the valleys of the south of the Island, so different from the cloudy skies over Guanajibo. That ceiling of reinforced concrete painted blue without a single cloud to darken the horizon was an ingenious affirmation of my parents' optimism in those years. They had an unshakable faith in a future built according to the forms of the American way of life. By contrast, the floors were made of alternating gray and yellow Puerto Rican tiles, as if they represented the constant change between days of sunny happiness and those of dark depression.

Both balconies—the North American and the Criollo—looked out over a garden that, like the Guanajibo garden, was also enclosed by a wall and required constant attention. They had to water the garden all the time since Ponce was in an eternal drought. Even though my mother spent much of her day taking care of it, the garden never had the romantic exuberance of the garden of Guanajibo, where it rained every day. The grass was its greatest luxury. It was carefully fertilized and manicured. For Father, that grass was a symbol of the control and discipline necessary against the temptations of Nature that invited you to dream and escape from reality. According to Father, the new positive and pragmatic status of the Island as a territory on the point of becoming part of the North American union was represented by that carefully cultivated and manicured garden. Unlike Guanajibo, it did not make you think of the Jauja Valley nor of the Amazon jungles of Hudson's novel *Green Mansions*. Instead it made you think of the desert gardens of Arizona and New Mexico.

The garden at La Alhambra represented a repression that was sexual rather than political (although there is nothing more political than the sexual). Father repeated every day at dinner time "Let's live a moral, upstanding life," quoting Eugenio María de Hostos. Mother echoed him to the letter.

Two faces from those years in the Alhambra house are profoundly etched in my memory: the face of Guanime, the Guatemalan, and Luz, the peasant from Jayuya.

Guanime was the first Latin American maid that came to Ponce with a green card. At that time the tuna processing plants and factories of electronic machines employed all the women from the slums where

Mother usually went looking for the help: Machuelo Abajo, Machuelito, and Cuatro Calles. During the suppers and lunch parties, there was only one topic of conversation among the women: the fact that now no maid wanted to work for less than a dollar an hour, how they all talked back, and insisted they were not "maids" but "employees," how during dinner they stuck their noses in what was clearly none of their business, how they answered with gross language when they were reprimanded, and even went so far as to refuse to wear uniforms with white collar and apron.

Mother had waited for Guanime for many months with the anticipation of the believer who waits for Divine Grace to free her from her household chores. My father and she had paid all expenses for the trip from Guatemala through an employment agency. They were prepared to pay any price to get permanent residency status for Guanime. Perhaps that time Mother's excessive expectations were due to her profound ignorance about Latin America. She was never interested in visiting there. We only discussed and read North American and European literature and history in the Alhambra house as if Latin America did not exist. In fact, there was no reason to think that a woman from Guatemala should be smarter and more efficient than any of the women from the poorer neighborhoods of Ponce. Yet my mother insisted that harmful North American values had not arrived in Guatemala, and their maids were still tame and obedient.

The day that Guanime arrived at the house was proof for me that a totally different universe existed south of the Tropic of Cancer. Guanime was probably the first Latin American Indian to arrive in Ponce. She was fat with a huge head that came out of her shoulders like an Olmec statue. She hardly spoke Spanish. She arrived wearing her Mayan wipil. She packed all her belongings in a yute sack. What impressed us the most were her feet. She had walked hundreds of miles from her village in the Sierra Madre de Chiapas to Guatemala City in her woven straw slippers. They looked like they would fall apart. But that did not bother Guanime because her feet had a thick layer of crust from years of walking that would make Saint Christopher, the saint of travelers, pale with envy. Her feet were wide and thick like those of an elephant. They were at least twelve inches long. My mother was astonished. Clearly, she did not expect that monster of a woman, who sat down at the servants' table on the balcony at the back of the house, and proceeded to clean out the entire pot of rice together with the pot of beans in one sitting. Since Guanime was already working on her fourth pork chop, my mother took her plate away and forbade the cook from making her another.

Obese people bothered Mother because being fat went against the aesthetic sensibility of Guanajibo. She was afraid it was going to be difficult to find a uniform that was big enough for Guanime in Ponce, so she decided to subject her to a strict diet. Mother put the pantry under lock and key and ordered the cook to serve her a small portion of rice and beans, one slice of fried plantain, and a salad for dinner. Guanime meekly obeyed her, except on one occasion when they brought a bunch of fifty manzano bananas, with their skins exploding open from the sheer sweetness of the fruit. They were forgotten and left on the servant's dinner table, and Guanime ate every last one all by herself.

In the end, Guanime lost weight and Mother made her wear one of the uniforms with white collar and lace apron. But she was not ready to show her off to her friends nor to let Guanime serve the hors d'oeuvres and beverages during afternoon snack. The biggest problem continued to be Guanime's feet, which were too large for any shoes. To have a servant in La Alhambra go barefoot at table was unthinkable, and my mother had combed the stores looking for shoes. Mother took Guanime to be fitted for all types of shoes without success. One day the solution dawned on me. I took Guanime to a sporting goods store and there we bought her a pair of Converse tennis shoes, size fourteen and a half, the same shoes that basketball players wore.

Luz María was another example of how my mother exercised absolute control in the Alhambra house. Luz was a young woman, tall and blond with delicate facial features that made everyone happy when she arrived at our house. She had a magic touch for cooking, but we always had to speak to her in whispers because everything scared her. At that time we had a live-in gardener named Manuel who had been working for us for many years. Manuel had jet black hair and copper-colored skin, high cheek bones, and teeth as white as a slice of soursop. He was a healthy young man who had also been born in the mountains near Indiera Fría. His father owned a small vegetable farm that was close to being bankrupt. My father had lent him money so that he would not lose the farm. In payment Don Manuel had sent us Rosa, Margarita, and Manuel, who was a gardener. My mother was crazy about him because he was very responsible and had a green thumb when it came to fruit trees, so much so that under his care the garden had become an orchard. One day my mother noticed something in Luz, perhaps a glance, or a subtle gesture when Manuel was around, which made her suspect that they were in love. She sent me to spy on them at night to see what they did when everyone else was sleeping. I remember that I took off my shoes and walked barefoot in the dark across the yard, avoiding the thorns of the lemon tree, arriving at the servants' quarters, which were in a separate building at the back of the property. There I peeked through one of the blinds and saw a scene that I will take to my grave. Together, the beautiful bodies of Luz (the color of mother of pearl) and Manuel (all muscles and the color of Cinnamon) made the figure of a star, a maranta swirl of gold and black breasts, arms, hands and legs, inside the small cement room, sweating profusely, oblivious to the world, celebrating their love in absolute silence. It was like a dream. Now I am sure that Mother did not know what was going on. If she had known, she would not have sent me to spy. She thought they were in love. Unfortunately, that night their flirting became a reality. Deeply ashamed, I returned to my room and went straight to bed. I felt dirty and corrupt not because I had seen their love-making but because I had seen it in those circumstances. I was angry at myself, because it was none of my business. When I got up the next morning, Mother did not say anything to me. She figured out just looking at me what I had seen. Mother fired Luz that very day, and Manuel left with her.

Manuel's sister Rosa was a proud young girl with apple-red cheeks and a black braid that went down to her waist. She was good-hearted and always ready to work. She worked for us for many years. She finally married and went to live in Machuelo Abajo, the slum along the banks of the Portugués River. Her younger sister Margarita was my age, around 10 years old, when she arrived at our house. She was supposed to be my playmate but also to take care of me. She was thin and small, of a weak constitution, and innocent like country folk. We became very good friends and I would worry about the oval-shaped mole she had on her forehead. It was two inches long and covered in hair. At first it frightened me because it looked like a cockroach. However, when I realized that she was distressed because of the mole, I felt bad and began a campaign to convince my parents to allow Margarita to remove her mole with an operation. We took her to the doctor, but his opinion was that the operation would be dangerous for her because the cyst was deep and because it was located on her forehead. I left for the United States to go to school when I was thirteen and I did not return until summer vacation. Margarita was no longer in the house. I missed her very much, but her father had come back for her and had taken her back to the country.

We had two chauffeurs in the house: Carmelo Bocachica, who was as black as coal, and Carmelo Martínez, who was white with green eyes. They took turns picking me up at school on Isabel Street at four o'clock driving the family's blue and white Cadillac. Carmelo was born at the Bocachica sugar mill that was located near Santa Isabel. He was always my favorite driver because he bought me snow cones after school. He was a happy person and loving so I called him chocolate Caramelo. Carmelo Martínez was serious and stern. I called him lemon Caramelo. Carmelo Bocachica worked for us for many years and when he retired, my father gave him the white Lincoln Continental instead of trading it in for a new car. For many years after that, Carmelo, at the wheel of his white Lincoln, became a feature of Ponce.

Now, many years later, I think of Gilda, of Rosa, of Margarita, of Manuel, and of Carmelo. I never knew anything more about them; they are like the flying embers after a big fire.

Uncle Nino, my mother's favorite brother, died in an airplane accident in 1942, and this made Mother terribly depressed. Six years after his death we still could not mention my uncle's name in front of my mother without a chilly silence entering the room, filling my mother's eyes with tears. She used to spend hours looking at the photo album where she had a few pictures of him, all that remained to remember him by. She had cut out his picture from all the family photographs so that he could sit floating at the bottom of the empty black page untouched by the proximity of his loved ones, especially of his widow, Aunt Ángeles. I still remember the bitter smile that I saw on my mother's face when I asked her one day why my aunt and cousins did not come to visit our house since we saw them every Sunday at the cemetery. Mother told me they did not come because she herself had forbidden it. Mother could not cope with the sadness of the memory of her brother's death.

If we went to the beach, she did not get in the water. On the day of my first communion my mother was still mourning her brother's death six years later. Instead of the colorful print on the first communion cards commemorating the event, mine were in black and white and written in funeral print.

Gilda Ventura came to pull me out of that well of sadness where I was drowning from Uncle Nino's death. I was seven years old. Gilda was no more than ten years older than I when she arrived at our house. She came from a family of fourteen children. No doubt, working for us assured her livelihood, and helped her and her family prevent hunger. Her work was strictly limited to keeping me safe and looking after me, which probably seemed extravagant to her, since her brothers, all younger than myself, ran around without shoes and half naked near the mangroves surrounding La Esperanza, one of the sugar mills of the Ponce valley close to Merceditas.

Gilda had a happy temperament. She dressed in print dresses that accentuated the lovely lines of her bronzed and supple body. I especially liked to watch her paint a bright red mouth over her thick brown lips with one expert stroke. Her name was, without a doubt, Italian in origin and even operatic, probably the result of the love of opera of a landowner from Ponce, who hired her father as a worker and was godfather to his daughter. Gilda always insisted that her name was spelled with a "G" and not with an "H," like the name of the hunchback's daughter in *Rigoletto* by Verdi. Some years later, when I went to the opera as an adolescent and saw the scene where Rigoletto discovers the wounded body of Gilda inside a burlap sack, after she sacrifices herself to Sparafucile's knife for the life of the duke, I couldn't stop myself from crying.

I felt that Gilda's betrayal of Rigoletto was a lesson about the dangers of loving a strange man, for whom, one day, we would abandon our home and the father we adored.

Gilda was not a light skinned blonde like Verdi's heroine. She was black, tall, and thin. Her skin reminded me of the copper bark of the almácigo, a birch tree that only grows on the southern coast of the Island, and where the rebellious souls of the Caribe Indians are said to live, according to popular legend. Gilda was happy and mouthy. She never kept quiet when my mother scolded her for giving me "Limbers" to eat. These were delicious frozen treats made with bright colored syrups that became popular after the famous aviator Charles

Lindbergh visited the Island. The "Limbers" were sold on Estrella Street from filthy push carts surrounded by flies.

Gilda had her own version of Nietzsche's philosophy for these occasions; she would solemnly repeat "what doesn't kill you makes you fat," meaning "what doesn't kill you makes you stronger," and she handed me the treat with a wink. Besides her flowered cotton dresses she wore a turban on her head of the same fabric. One day I jokingly asked her if that decoration was her idea or if she was trying to copy Aunt Jemima from the pancake and waffle boxes that had invaded the kitchens of Ponce under the growing influence of the United States. Very seriously she answered that it was not a decoration; the women of San Antón wore the headdress because it made it easier to carry on their heads the big tubs of lard they used to bring water to their homes. I learned many things with Gilda; that, for example, not all the music in the world was classical and instrumental, but that there was another kind of music that not only spoke to you, but allowed you to talk back; that not everybody had running water in their home, and could afford to leave the faucet open for half an hour while you cleaned your hands. In short, thanks to Gilda, I learned that I did not live in California, or in Spain, but in Latin America.

Gilda found two ways of teaching me history. First, she began to take me to the movies with her every Saturday when it was her afternoon off. Instead of going to the Vermouth showing at the Fox Delicias movie theatre in Ponce's Plaza Degetau, where all the friends of my family went to see movies like *The Temple of the Gods* with Johnny Weismuller or *East of Eden* with James Dean, we secretly went to what my family referred to as "meaitos:" dingy movie theatres like the Metro or the Habana, where we had to be careful not to sit under the cheap seats, for fear of the spittle that could slowly descend on our heads, green and large like a jellyfish in December.

There I discovered a world until then unknown to me. It was the world of María Félix, Pedro Infante, Agustín Lara, José Alfredo Jiménez, and Jorge Negrete. Until that moment I thought English was the language of the movie stars, since James Mason and Ava Gardner in *The Flying Dutchman* spoke in that language, and so did Clark Gable and Grace Kelly in *Mogambo*. Gilda's preference for Mexican movies led her to make me a very special scrapbook. Gilda cut pictures of María Félix, Libertad Lamarque, and Dolores del Río from the pages of *Vanidades* magazine, and together we attached them to a marble composition notebook with a thick paste of flour and water. I was obsessed by María Felix's nails, above all. They were incredibly long and red. Mother would never let her nails grow like that, nor would any of the North American movie actresses like Doris Day or Grace Kelly that she used as examples because they were refined, blond, and well educated. Nevertheless I loved the nails of María Felix and her abundant and disheveled jet black hair, and I found her much more attractive than the scrawny Hollywood actresses.

One Sunday night, a few weeks after I saw my first Mexican movie, Gilda made me listen to Quiñones Vidal's *Noticiero radial* on radio station WNEL. I then discovered there was another type of music very different from what was played in the living room at home. I became a fan of that program, and I would sing with Gilda, at all hours of the day, María Grever and Pedro Vargas's boleros. The first poems I ever heard in my life were the songs *Júrame, Cuando vuelva a tu lado, Volveré, Por unos ojazos negros, Estrellita, Solamente una vez, Flores negras, Piénsalo bien, Noche de ronda,* Ódiame, and *Ojos malvados,* and I got to know them thanks to Gilda.

Other nights Gilda and I listened to Felipe Rodríguez, known as "the voice," on WNEL radio. Felipe was a jíbaro, a peasant from the mountains of Caguas. He had a pencil-thin mustache, hair styled with Glostora, a tight-fitting smoking jacket rented by the hour, and a nasal, gravelly voice that in those days had taken the Island by storm. He had become famous singing at the Palladium in New York with his trio Los Antares, and when the Korean War broke out in 1950, he was the national hero of Puerto Ricans shipping out every day from New York. *La última copa,* a melancholic and nostalgic tango, became the song of the 65th Infantry Regiment. Felipe sang that tango in every single farewell:

> Pour me a glass, my friend,
> and just keep pouring until
> It overflows with champagne
> On this night of revelry and happiness
> I want to drown all my sorrows
> It's the last celebration of my life
> Of a life, my friends, that's about to end,
> Better yet, a life that has gone after one,
> Who could never return my love.

The tango had no charm; the lyrics could not compare to those of *Júrame* or *Noche de ronda*, for example. It made no obvious reference to the reality of Puerto Ricans at the time. However, the verse "It's the last celebration of my life, of a life, my friends, that's about to end" did imply the tragedy of shipping out to a war in Asia that had nothing to do with them. Other compositions that followed Felipe's *La última copa* were played on the radio and alluded to the Korean War: Daniel Santos's *Carta* and Bobby Capó's *Nuestro regimento*, which became the *Marcha del 65*. And it was no coincidence that the 65th Infantry Regiment was decommissioned at that time, nor was it by chance that its troops were reassigned to other Army regiments after the Korean War. In short, the songs that Gilda and I heard on the radio cleared the walls of purple bougainvillea of my house and turned the Korean War into an undeniable reality.

Quiñones Vidal played another kind of music on his radio program, songs like the *plenas* that alluded to the explosive reality of that time. The *plena* is a song similar to the Mexican *corrido*. Its function is to inform the listeners of an event or a sensational piece of news that is relevant to the listener. Gilda was from San Antón and she loved *plenas*. It was thanks to her that I first listened to *Mamita llegó el Obispo*.

The last year that Gilda worked for us was 1960. It was an election year, and the political landscape promised an out-and-out fight between the assimilationist party that was in power, and the Catholic bishops, Monsignors Innes and MacManus, who had sponsored a new political party, the *Partido de Acción Cristiana* (Christian Action Party) or PAC. Monsignor MacManus, the bishop who had founded the University of Santa María, took the initiative during the campaign. He was a tremendously active man who was full of energy and was responsible for many acts of charity among the poor of Ponce. He also lived in La Alhambra in a villa in the Spanish style very similar to ours. He said Mass every Sunday in a chapel he had built for himself next to the villa. The house had previously belonged to the Oppenheimer family and had a truculent history that surrounded the bishop with the beatific aura of one who blessed bad places and dispensed peace on troubled marriages. One of the darkest tragedies of Ponce happened in that house.

Jorge Oppenheimer was married to Rosina Sánchez, a woman well known in Ponce for her beauty. Jorge had gone on a trip, and when he returned unexpectedly to the house, he surprised his wife in the arms of her lover. He jerked her out of bed, pulled her along the red tile hallway and down the luxurious latticed-banister stairway, and threw her out of the house, shooting her three times in the back while the unfortunate woman ran terrified through the garden. Furious with jealousy, Jorge went back to the house, went upstairs, and killed the unlucky lover on the balcony, and then killed himself with a shot to the head.

Because of this tragedy, the Oppenheimer house in La Alhambra remained closed for many years, a den of vandals and hoodlums, until the bishop bought it and celebrated a Mass of the dead in it during which he publicly conferred peace on Jorge and Rosina's souls even though Jorge had committed suicide. After Mass the bishop celebrated an Easter Sunday breakfast at the house as the entire population of Ponce walked in front of the beautiful balcony where the crime had been committed. People whispered that the balcony—which Jorge Oppenheimer had had copied from the movie *Sunset Boulevard* where Gloria Swanson shot William Holden, before he fell into the swimming pool—had been the real cause of the tragedy. In memory of the event and in order to prove to the inhabitants of La Alhambra that adulterous blood had been washed forever from those floors, the bishop had built in the garden the Chapel of the Bishopric decorated with some excellent murals in the style of Diego Rivera, a work of Vela Zanetti, a Catalan painter who had a common-law marriage with a *jíbara* near the Tetas de Cayey. In them were portrayed idyllic scenes of the Puerto Rican countryside with *jíbaros* cutting sugar cane, pulling tobacco, and picking coffee beans. But since Governor Luis Muñoz Marín had just been elected by the very same *jíbaros* on a socialist platform, those murals were like a visual hemetic for the parishioners from La Alhambra who, dressed in their Sunday best, attended mass in the purified home of the Oppenheimers.

The PPD had tried to control the population of the Island by supporting the use of contraceptives, but the effort enraged the bishops who had founded the PAC. Soon the yellow and white flags of the bishops' party began to shoot up on the television antennas of all the houses, and the slums looked like loyal armies mobilized for a new Crusade. Some months before the election Bishop MacManus gave out leaflets that said "the PPD has been an enemy of Catholic ideals for many years." The scandal grew when he sent a pastoral letter to the diocese and gave a sermon in the Cathedral where he warned that anyone voting for Governor Muñoz Marín would be *ipso facto* excommunicated from the Catholic church. Even though what led MacManus to take these actions was the support of the pro-assimilation Party for family planning, the gossip in La Alhambra suggested a different reason. They said that MacManus had privately accused the governor of living "out of wedlock" with his wife before marrying her, and this morally disqualified him for his post. The governor was looking for an issue that would give his re-election campaign a boost, and MacManus's absurd accusation was like manna from heaven.

As soon as Gilda learned what was going on between the governor and the bishop, she began to turn the dial on our radio, every night with increasing resolve. "You just wait and see," she said to me, "the shit is going to hit the fan." And so it did. A few days later we heard for the first time on the radio the *plena Mamita llegó el Obispo,* and it went like this:

> *Mamita* the bishop is here.
> The bishop arrived from Rome.
> *Mamita*, if you saw him,
> You would want to take him home!

> They say he doesn't drink rum,
> But he drinks it by the barrel.
> *Mamita*, if you saw him,
> You would want to take him home!

> The bishop plays cards and gambles,
> He gets drunk and falls in love.
> *Mamita*, if you saw him,
> You would want to take him home!

> But the little convent sisters
> sisters of the Sacred Heart
> warn the ladies to be careful
> For that bishop is a shark!

The Partido Popular Democrático won the election by a whopping 456,000 votes; the triumph resulted in the excommunication from the Catholic church of half the population of the Island. Sometime later Bishop MacManus left the Island for good when his superiors ordered him to return to the diocese of New York.

When I married and left Ponce, I lost all contact with Gilda. I do not know how she found me, but one day she came to see me at my house in San Juan. She was dressed in white with a blue sash attached at the waist indicating that she was betrothed to Christ. She had lost her former ruddy complexion but she treated me with her usual kindness. She told me she had married and had six children, that her husband had gone to New York and left her, and that now she had to raise and educate her children all by herself. She was also gravely ill. She had been diagnosed with cancer and needed an operation. When I offered to pay the costs, she assured me that it was not necessary, that the doctors at the Municipal Hospital, founded during the government of Muñoz Marín, would operate for free, but that she needed to ask me a favor. When I asked her what it was, she laughed with that powerful laugh of hers, throwing her head back, and told me, "I want you to donate a bell to my church in the barrio de San Antón. You already know how much I like music, and if I have to die, I want God to know that I did not keep quiet, not even in the hour of my death."

The house in La Alhambra had a third balcony, also made from wrought iron balusters, that belonged to the guest room and that was almost completely surrounded by an enormous jasmine vine that climbed to the roof. It was a narrow balcony, made almost secret by the fact that in order to stand on it you first had to open the doors to the balcony until they hit the balusters. Then, you had to close the French doors one at a time while standing between them. I was very thin so I would slip between the doors, closing them behind me with great difficulty, remaining isolated in a grotto that floated between the silence of a bedroom that was rarely opened or cleaned and the warm pool of grass under my feet.

After Gilda left the house, suffering the same fate as the other maids, I started locking myself in the guest room balcony. There I spent hours sitting on the floor reading comic books or the novels I stole from my father's library, many of which were on the Catholic church's index of forbidden books. Meanwhile I heard the maids

looking for me all through the house to make me eat, take a bath, or practice my piano lesson. Even though I loved stories since I was a child, I do not remember my mother ever reading one to me or even telling me one. But from that balcony that remained secret forever I enjoyed the indiscriminate pageant of Emma Bovary, Doña Bárbara, Nancy Drew, Cathy Heathcliff, Jane Eyre, Charlotte and Emily Brönte, Milady, Becky Sharp, Wonder Woman, Sheena, Jane and Chita, Juliet, Cordelia, Goneril and Reagan, Little Lulu, Joan of Arc, and Scheherezade, whose unexpurgated version of *A Thousand and One Nights* was snatched away from me unceremoniously one day when I asked my grandmother, Mamita Pepé, why the Arabian brides shaved their pubis on their wedding day "until it was left smooth like the palm of the hand."

My father was a marvelous person; he was caring, gentle, brilliant. This does not mean that he was not a disciplinarian, but he was an iron hand inside a silk glove. When he was with me, I felt happy; the sun shone and there were no clouds that threatened the horizon. Father was a man of action and very optimistic; he always had so many projects that he would have needed two lives to complete them.

But when I was with Mother I felt sad. Her life was taking care of us and the house. We used to spend a lot of time in the garden. She loved dogs, and on one occasion when our pointer gave birth to seven pups, we took our picture with them on our laps.

Her master's in History didn't amount to anything. She never practiced her chosen profession. She never returned to the classroom once she married Father even though she was a voracious reader and kept abreast of all the most recent Latin American and Puerto Rican authors. The day I gave her *Cien años de soledad* (*One Hundred Years of Solitude* by Gabriel García Márquez) she said: "Those were one hundred years of desolation, not solitude." She was a friend of the writer Abelardo Díaz Alfaro and even gave the name of Abelardo to a Puerto Rican rooster that wandered in the garden. She exchanged letters with him and commented on his radio program. But to live in Ponce, where there was no nourishing intellectual life, made her sad. Her interests revolved around the house, the garden, and the piano that was her only hobby. Mother played the piano every afternoon and she loved Chopin's nocturnes, which filled me with melancholy. I felt like Chopin in the Cartuja de Valldemosa; spitting blood on the piano keys; breathing with difficulty the warm air of the terrace, where I studied every after-

Lorencita and Rosario with puppies

noon and felt like I was asphyxiating. I escaped from her by reading books by Edgar Rice Burroughs. As soon as Mother began to play preludes on the piano, I ran to find the four volumes of Tarzan and locked myself up with him and Jane in the forest of my bedroom.

I studied a lot in school, but I was bored during the summer. My parents never encouraged me to prepare for a career and thought that my destiny was simply to marry. I took the path of least resistance. We went on splendid trips to Europe. The trips we took are some of my best memories. Mother was afraid to fly since her brother's accident, and we would always travel by boat to the United States, on a cargo ship from the Taurus or Bull Lines that only had three or four state rooms for passengers. There was nothing to do, and we used to take dominoes and Parcheesi or books to read to entertain ourselves. We would reach Miami and from there traveled to Jacksonville, where we boarded a train to New York. One time aboard the train, Father realized that all the rest of the passengers were black and he went to ask the purser why that was. The purser answered him that that train was segregated and that since we were Puerto Rican, we could not sit with

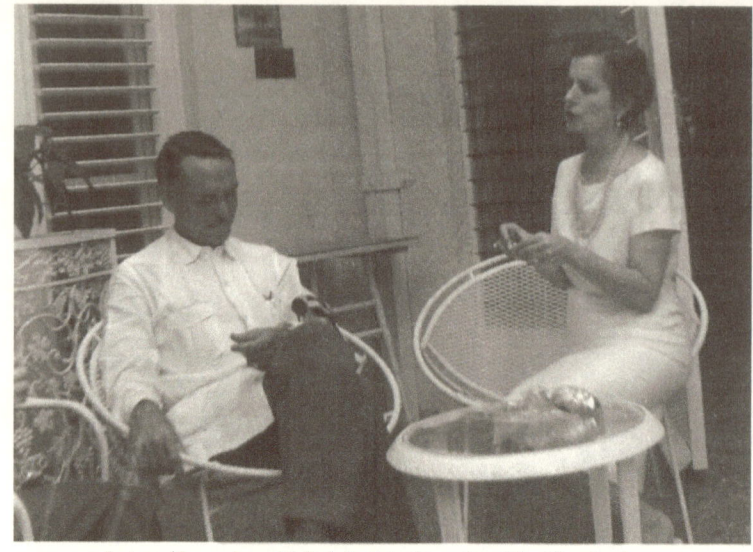

Luis and Lorencita, with little birds in the garden of the Alhambra house

Rosario, Lorencita, and Mister Cornell in the garden of the Alhambra house

*Rosario Ferré dressed in the uniform for the Sagrado Corazón School
in the garden of the Alhambra house*

whites. Father became angry and almost throttled the man. He asked
to see the conductor, who finally let us ride in a car for white people.
It was much more luxurious than the car for blacks, and the seats were
not cane seats but red velvet. This happened in the 1940s well before
desegregation. The experience made me aware that railroad stations
had segregated drinking fountains and bathrooms for blacks, and this
left me traumatized.

Between 1950 and 1960 we went to Europe four times. It took us
three days to get to Florida by boat, and then one additional night by
train. Once in New York, we boarded a cruise ship that took six or sev-
en days to get to Europe. Our first trip was on the *Stratheaven*, a British
ship that was already quite old. That was in 1950 when I was eleven and
my brother fifteen. We disembarked in Calais and there took a train to
Paris. Father constantly told us that we should not forget how fortunate we were, that it took him forty years to get to Europe and that we
were only eleven and fifteen and we were already there.

For Father and Mother, Europe was the fount of all culture and
civilization. "A trip to Europe is worth a year at university," said Mother.
My brother and I looked at her in amazement, and wanted to see every
single museum and church. Those trips started our thirst for knowledge.

The Ferré-Ramírez de Arellano family in the ship's dining room

In Paris we stayed at the Hotel Crillon on the Place Vendôme in front of the place where the guillotine used to sit, and where now stood an Egyptian obelisk placed there by Napoleon, according to Father. We spent two weeks in Paris visiting all the marvelous sights, and when we returned to the hotel completely worn out, I played with my jax ball, keeping it suspended in the jet of water from the bidet. I had never seen a bidet, and my mother did not explain what it was for. She only said that it was something that French women used to clean themselves "down under" since they did not often take baths. And it was true because at that time the French stank. During guided tours in museums, we had to fall behind so as not to drown in their smell. "That's why they invented perfume," Father would say, upset that Mother spoke badly of the French because his grandfather was also French.

Afterwards we went to Switzerland by train. We visited Geneva and climbed Mont Blanc and the Jungfrau. We visited Berne and Lausanne. From Switzerland we went to Rome, where we spent another week visiting wonders. We visited the Vatican on a guided tour with other people. We had an audience with Pope Pius XII. Mother and I took a photograph of ourselves, our eyes full of tears. In 1950 no one knew that Pope Pius XII was a fascist sympathizer. We visited the Vatican Museum, and we saw the tomb of the Emperor Hadrian, now called the Castel Sant'Angelo. We went to dozens of marvelous churches and of course to St. Peter's; we went up to the cupola, ignoring vertigo in order to see the splendid view of Rome from the roof of the basilica. On our return we visited Florence, where Father lost his head with the paintings he saw in the Piti Palace and the Uffizi Gallery. I suspect that it was there he decided to found a museum in Ponce even though that dream would have to wait thirty more years to become a reality.

In Florence I had a memorable experience. Father wanted to commission a white marble bust of me, and I went with Mother to the workshop of Antonio Frilli. I posed for him one day. They had to take a photograph of me because we would not be in Florence for very long and the sculptor needed the photo to finish the bust. They took me to a room where they photographed the models. The sculptor began to call me "carina bambina," and after taking a picture of my face, he insisted on a picture of me in the nude. I ran out of the room, took my mother away from there, and we returned to the hotel. In the end, the sculptor made the bust, and it is rather good even if it is after a single photo.

I believe it was in Marseilles that we waited for a limousine with uniformed chauffeur who would drive us to Gibraltar, because to travel by train in Spain at that time was impossible. The trains were antiquated and very slow. The Civil War had left Spain in poverty. The limousine had cartouche seats; in other words it had seats that could be removed so that five people would fit comfortably in the back. It had a rack on the roof for luggage that was strapped in with rope. Because we packed for a three-month-long trip we had a lot of luggage and it did not fit in the trunk.

It had been twelve years since the end of the Civil War in 1939, and Spain lived more or less twenty years behind the rest of Europe. As we drove through the small towns, especially in

Photo of Rosario used as a reference by the sculptors in Florence

the south of Spain, all the neighbors and even the older people came out of their houses to see our limousine. The food was terrible, everything cooked in rancid oil and of poor quality; we ate boiled eggs so that we would not get sick to our stomach. It was very sad to see that beautiful Spain, so full of history and culture and ethnically diverse, but we couldn't do anything for them. They were proud to the very oldest one, skin as wrinkled as parchment paper, silently watching us drive by, never begging for money. At that time Spain had a particular odor; it smelled of old, of millennial dust, of rancid oil, and of clothes that were out-of-style in the United States. Madrid was a sad city of buildings covered with soot with monuments everywhere to Primo de Rivera and Generalísimo Francisco Franco.

We stayed at the Ritz, which was a good hotel then but not as expensive as it is today. I remember that neither bullfighters nor movie actors were allowed to stay there.

On our way from Madrid to Seville something else happened that was memorable. I had asked that my parents buy me a Mariquita Pérez doll from Galerías Preciado. It came in a trunk filled with doll clothes made by the expert hands of Spanish seamstresses. Mariquita was at least two feet tall and was made of caramel-colored hard plastic paste. She was what the Spanish called morena, of dark hair and eyes. In the car, I began to talk about the doll, which had cost the equivalent of $200 in Spanish pesetas. The driver heard me, stopped the car in the middle of the road, and got out, furious. On foot, by himself, he left us behind sitting in the car with our mouths open. Father got out of the car and ran after him asking for an explanation, and the driver told him he did not want to drive people around Spain who wasted the annual wages of a worker on a Mariquita Pérez. They talked for a while by the side of the road until the man calmed down and returned to the car. I never found out what Father said to him, but from that moment on my embarrassment was so great that I did not take the doll out of its trunk again until we left Spain.

We returned to New York from Gibraltar, where we boarded the *Conte Bianca Mano*, an Italian cruise ship. The bust of Rosarito was stored in the hold, packed in a wooden crate. We arrived in Puerto Rico a few weeks later.

The trips we made between 1954 and 1960 were just as interesting. We traveled on the *Queen Mary* and the *Andrea Doria*, the most beautiful of all. The walls and the ceiling of the state rooms were decorated with constellations, and the balusters of the stairways going up and down between decks were made from Murano glass. Some years later the ship sank in a tragic accident. Whenever I remember it, I can see fish swimming between the beautiful balusters.

On later trips, we traveled to Germany, adding to our itinerary. We always went to Italy to see the works of art, but now went to Naples and Capri, Rome again, then Florence and Milan. We travelled from Marseilles to Spain by car. In order to return from France, one time we went through Burgos up Biarritz to Paris and then Calais. Other times we left through Vigo, where we boarded the *Antilles*. Leaving from Vigo was very convenient because we traveled directly to San Juan, which made the trip much shorter, and it was more fun because the ship was full of Puerto Ricans.

These trips were like oases where we drank every three or four years. During the rest of the summer my most important activity was to attend dances at the Casino and at Escambrón and private parties thrown by my new friends from San Juan, dressed in Luisa Matienzo gowns, a San Juan designer who was famous at that time for her extravagant dresses that made you look like a doughnut wrapped in sequins, beads, and rhinestones. It was the type of evening wear that was in style, especially among middle class young women from the towns of the Island. The sophisticated young women of San Juan society no longer wore that kind of dress, preferring instead simple designs by Dior or Givenchi that they bought in Saks Fifth Avenue and Bergdorf Goodman. But I was just a hick, a jíbara, and was very happy with my dresses of petals and puffs.

We also went on short trips to the island of Caja de Muertos in the family yacht, *El Patoño*, where I had a wonderful time. But when I returned home sunburnt and plastered in Noxzema, with my hair wet and light after washing off a ton of sand, I felt a hole in my soul, an emptiness where I suffocated. The price I paid for those luxuries was my freedom, and at home they never lost sight of me. I was under constant supervision and I was never sent to summer camp. My ballet classes in Bill Zarazin and Evelyn Tristan's academy thrilled me, but when I turned fifteen, they took me out because I had to dance with men. When I went to the Club Deportivo to play basketball or tennis, I was always chaperoned by an employee.

Rosario Ferré as a member of the Dana Hall fencing team

Around 1950 my parents heard rumors that the Latin American nuns at the Colegio de las Madres did not teach English well, and, to top it all off, that they tried to fill my head with their nonsense. I was very pious and at that time I prayed and went to Mass every Sunday. My grandfather, who was a Mason, began to worry that the nuns were filling the heads of the girls with dreams of heroism and holiness, and that the nuns tried to catch them with their siren song, hoping to turn girls into nuns and increase their numbers at the convent. That was what happened with Titi Iso, my grandfather said. My parents were warned. And my life was completely changed.

Father and Mother decided to send me to study at Dana Hall when I was thirteen, a boarding school for young women in Massachusetts. I ended up in a Calvinist school just as strict as our house at La Alhambra, but I never lost faith. I still prayed Our Father and Hail Mary every night, and I was free for the first time in my life. I learned that one can be a prisoner in a cell, but there are no limits to our mind, and once we begin to think nobody can tell us to stop. My life was schizophrenic: nine months of the year I lived in a Spartan dormitory in New England; I attended vespers services every Friday; I read at random Luther, Milton, the St. James Bible, and the works of Shakespeare; I studied biology and astronomy; I learned not only that man descended from the ape but that Planet Earth probably is not the only stellar body with life in the universe. I was a member of the fencing team for three years and won the gold medal in a competition in Massachusetts. When I graduated, I went to Wellesley College and later to Manhattanville College in Purchase, New York, where I graduated in 1960. There, I went everywhere by myself. Weekends I took the train to New York City to go to the opera or the theatre, and I stayed alone in hotels whenever I pleased.

But when I returned to Ponce for summer vacation, I went to Mass every Sunday with my parents, and I declared that we were children of Adam and Eve and that only Catholics could be saved and go to heaven. In Ponce I slept in a room with French furniture and Venetian lamps, I pretended to be interested only in clothes and parties that bored me, and hypocritically I let them chaperone me everywhere.

These are the memories of my life in Ponce before I moved to San Juan in 1960 and began a totally different life. Being Puerto Rican and Antillean, I carry in me the memory of a Corsican great grandfather, of a French great great grandfather who emigrated to Cuba and later to Panama to build the Canal with Ferdinand de Lesseps, of a great grandfather who went blind and later supported himself by selling lottery tickets, of a great great grandfather from Castile and another from Cordoba, who emigrated to the Island to seek their fortune. All of them loved and suffered on the Island, and they are all buried in Puerto Rico.

NOTES

1. Before this the Sagrado school was located in the former Girls Asylum on Ponce de León Avenue. The school moved to its current location in Santurce in 1907.

How I Began to Write

Writing is a mystery that I still do not understand. It is a gift we receive at birth. Ideas come from the darkness where we began and where we return when we fall asleep.

Literature does not have anything to do with life and yet it has everything to do with it. I never would have become a writer if, in 1960, I had not left Ponce and moved to San Juan. That year, I graduated from Manhattanville College and married Benigno Trigo. We had three children: Rosario Lorenza, Benigno Luis, and Luis Alfredo. All three have been wonderful children; they have always supported me and have been my guides during the difficult moments of my life. They have been my most important achievement: they are upstanding citizens with integrity and they contribute to society with their chosen careers; and they do so with humanity and generosity of spirit. All of my achievements do not compare to my children, who led difficult lives because of my struggle to free myself from social conventions that put limits and boundaries on life.

I have lived in San Juan at 66 Marbella Street since 1965. Enrique Vivoni recently found the blueprints to my house while researching the old houses in Condado. He discovered that my house was designed by Pedro de Castro. I have a close identification with my house. When I restored it more than 40 years ago, I had a terrace built with old, large balusters shaped like amphorae. The balusters belonged to a house in Ponce that was torn down. When Mother passed by it in her car, and

Rosario Ferré and her three children, Benigno, Rosaloren, and Luis at the Marbella house

saw the balusters thrown in the rubble, she rescued them and stored them in the garage of our Alhambra house. When I remodeled my house on Marbella Street, she gave them to me as a gift. I spend most of my day reading, writing, and dreaming in that terrace. It is a place where the eastern breeze always blows, the trade winds of my stories. That is why, even though I live in San Juan, I feel like I brought a little piece of Ponce with me.

During the sixties, I was a traditional homemaker. In 1970 I enrolled in the Hispanic Studies Program at the University of Puerto Rico to take a course on Garcilaso de la Vega with Professor Margot Arce de Vázquez. I majored in English and French literature at Manhattanville College. When my younger son turned 3, I decided to get a Masters in Spanish literature. The University of Puerto Rico did not give me transfer credit for the courses I took in the United States, so it would take twice the regular amount of courses to finish my degree. I did not become discouraged, and I began working toward my master's even if it meant taking only one course per semester. My responsibilities as a wife and mother of three children made it impossible for me to spend more time in class. I received a classical education in the Hispanic Studies Department. Some of my professors were Arce de Vázquez, Manuel Porras Cruz, Pablo García Díaz, Enrique Laguerre, Luis Arrigoitía, José Ramón de la Torre, Federico Acevedo, Arcadio Díaz Quiñones, Francisco Manrique Cabrera, Ángel Rama, and Mario Vargas Llosa. It was a wonderful time, one of stimulating intellectual growth. Students who later became distinguished writers, professors, and intellectuals such as Esteban Tollinchi, Luce and Mercedes López-Baralt, Olga Nolla, Edgardo Rodríguez Juliá, and Hugo Rodríguez Vecchini were my peers in the course on The Techniques of the Novel taught by Vargas Llosa.

In 1969, I wrote my first short story, "La caja de cristal," on a Royal or Royalite portable typewriter that was so light it would slide off the table, and I had to hold on to it as I typed. I contracted mononucleosis and was ordered to stay in bed for two or three weeks. I was bored from staring at the walls so I took out the Royal from its black case and I put it on a breakfast tray that I used as a table in bed. "La caja de cristal" became one of the stories in *Papeles de Pandora*, published in 1976.

Rosario Ferré with a poster of Zona. Carga y Descarga

But my career as a writer really started in 1970 when I began to work with a group of writers and we published *Zona. Carga y descarga*. Ángel Rama was its godfather. My cousin Olga Nolla and I had literary ambitions, and he advised us that the best thing would be for us to start our own literary journal. And so

Rosario and Olga working on Zona. Carga y Descarga *in Zilia Sánchez's apartment*

we did. The first volume of *Zona* came out in 1972. We sold the journal for fifty cents a piece in university hallways, bookstores, and even in the streets of Río Piedras. We typeset it ourselves with Zilia Sánchez, who helped to give the journal an Avant Garde look. My son Benigno published an essay in 2009 where he talks about Zilia's important contribution:

> "The fact that Sánchez's principle of design outlasted her partici-pation in the first three or four numbers of the journal, also suggests her profound influence on it. This principle can perhaps be summarized as the notion of the page as both a tactile and visual art object and agent, as something more than a neutral and passive space that merely contained the more important writing and images. Instead, *Zona*'s page was a signifying space in itself; it gave support to the intersecting and parallel planes of color, type, and image; and it stretched the possibilities of the materials. This principle was never abandoned, as is evident from its gradual stylization until the last number of the journal."

With *Zona*, something else happened that was very important for me: I became aware of our political situation and decided that independence was the only solution to our problems. In the courses on Puerto Rican literature taught at the Hispanic Studies Department, we only read writers who cried for independence: José de Diego, Gautier Benítez, and Lloréns Torres. It was impossible not to fall in love with that ideal. But going from words to deeds was another matter, and when my cousin Olga Nolla and I came out in support of independence in an editorial in *Zona* 2, many people who bought it were furious. When *Zona* 8 came out with the erotic short story "El esclavo y el señor" by Manuel Ramos Otero, we heard that people bought the journal and burned it in their yards as if it were a thing from the devil. My political views have changed since then, and today I think that the United States is made up of many peoples and ethnicities, and that it is not impossible to become a Puerto Rican state.

Olga Nolla was very important to the journal. My relationship with her is much older than *Zona*. We were first cousins, and we spent a lot of time together from the time we were five or six. We were born in the same year and in the same month.

Olga Nolla with Rosario Ferré

I spent vacations in her house in Cerro de las Mesas in Mayagüez, where we explored the woods around the property. We went together to the movies and read a lot of comic and adventure books. She also spent time in my house, where we went to the Club Deportivo and rode horseback in the Serallés' property at the Central Merceditas. One time, the cinch on Olga's horse was not properly tied, and the saddle slipped, throwing Olga into the sugar cane field. With her extraordinary determination, she got back on the horse and kept riding. Miraculously she was not hurt. When we turned 16, we each had our coming out party. Mine was in my house in La Alhambra. Hers was in the Mayagüez Shooting Club.

Olga Nolla with Rosario Ferré

Rosario Ferré's sixteenth birthday party at the Alhambra house

We met again at Manhattanville College. Olga studied biology, and I studied literature. We belonged to the same circle of friends: Tere Picó, Ivonne Acosta, Carmen Mercedes Guerra, Margarita Pumarada, Olga, and I. We always sat together at a table in the dining hall. I remember once we were making noise playing music on the glasses and plates, and singing at the top of our lungs when Mother Brady, the general director, came over to us and told us that if we continued behaving like that, she would send us out of the dining hall "to join the Puerto Ricans in the kitchen." Perhaps today we would have gone to the kitchen to show our support of the Puerto Rican dishwashers and cooks, but it was 1960 and we didn't do anything like that. We were furious, got up from the table, and left the dining hall. Another time, something else happened that shows that prejudice against Puerto Ricans was everywhere. To go to New York, we had to take a bus that brought us to the train station in Purchase. On the bus, I started chatting with passengers who spoke Spanish and turned out to be

Olga Nolla and Rosario Ferré at Manhattanville (1958)

Puerto Rican. They said that they worked at Manhattanville College. When we arrived in Purchase, we said goodbye and went our separate ways. When I returned to Manhattanville College the next day, I found a note ordering me to go to the office, where they told me it was strictly forbidden to fraternize with the help in Spanish and that what I had done on the bus was wrong. I was told not to do it again if I did not want to be expelled from college. Shaking with fear, I told Brady that I would speak with anyone I pleased, in English or in Spanish.

Olga and I graduated that same year and on the following we both got married and then became mothers. We spent a lot of time together taking care of our babies. Olga used to live on the first floor in the San Jorge apartment building and was married to Carlos Conde. While we changed diapers, we would talk about the four volumes we had read by Arnold J. Toynbee. When her children were four or five years old, Olga also enrolled as a graduate student in the Hispanic Studies Program at the UPR, and we took many classes together: the Theory of the Novel, taught by Ángel Rama; History of a Deicide, a class taught by Vargas Llosa on the work of García Márquez—this course was the basis for the book that Vargas Llosa published several years later with the same title, though after a fist fight with García Márquez, on account of his wife, Patricia, Vargas Llosa pulled the book from the market; and The Poetry of César Vallejo, taught by Ángel Rama. During that time Olga was already writing. She had finished her first book, *De lo familiar*. She gave the book to Ángel Rama to read and he loved it. With his recommendation she was able to get it published in 1973 with Ediciones Dead Weight Press, in Buenos Aires, and with a prologue by Ángel.

I also wrote poetry at that time and was green with envy. I always tried to show Olga my poems, and I wanted Olga to show me hers, but she was always jealous of her work and never would show me anything she was writing. I felt unhappy because I sensed that she thought I wanted to copy her. I resented her for that for a long time. Not long after this, I wrote "La muñeca menor." I showed the story to Ángel, and he was delighted with it. His enthusiasm gave me self-confidence, and I began to write in earnest. Since we needed material to fill the pages of *Zona*'s first volume, I published "La muñeca menor" there, and later many other things.

My husband was very conservative, very "Spanish," and he was upset by *Zona* and by my persistence in taking classes at the University of Puerto Rico to launch a literary career. He was not opposed to my taking a course here and there as long as it was a hobby, like playing bridge for example, but when he saw I was in earnest, he became upset. I was not prepared to give in, even though I was taking classes at the slow rate of one course per semester. I realize now that the Avant Garde layout of *Zona*, with its brazen art and radical texts often written in a shocking language, was for him something intolerable. After some turbulent months we decided to divorce. It was a painful process, but because I was so wrapped up in my studies, I was able to overcome the devastating depression that lasted for several years.[1]

I traveled to Mexico in 1975 to look for material for the journal and there I met the Mexican writer Jorge Aguilar Mora. I also visited Editorial Era Press and submitted for consideration the manuscript for *Papeles de Pandora* to its editor, Neus Espresate, but she rejected it. During that same trip, I went to see don Joaquín Díez-Canedo at Mortiz Press, and he accepted my manuscript enthusiastically. He published *Papeles de Pandora* in 1976. All of my work from *Zona. Carga y descarga* is published in *Papeles*, and it appears in the same order I wrote it.

Jorge returned to Puerto Rico with me, and we married in San Juan in 1976. We were married by a judge in the home of the attorney Abraham Díaz González. When the ceremony began, the judge asked Jorge if he believed in God. He replied no. The judge immediately took off her robe and said she could not marry us because she did not marry atheists. Dismayed, Abraham asked Jorge if he believed that Jesus Christ had been a great man. Jorge said yes. The judge agreed with that response and continued with the wedding.

Not too long after that, my children and I went to live in Mexico. There I wrote the book of feminist essays *Sitio a Eros*. Editorial Joaquín Mortiz Press also published it. The book came out in two editions, the second one considerably expanded. It included essays on Sylvia Plath, Flora Tristán, Mary Shelley, Alexandra Kollontay, and other rebellious and passionate women with sentimental problems. I took the title from an essay by the Russian feminist Alexandra Kollontay titled *Sitio a Eros alado*, published in 1923. In my book, the title *Sitio a Eros* is ambiguous. It means that one should give space to eroticism in life but at the same time one should try to control it. This book sold well in Mexico and Puerto Rico. At times women approached me to say that the book had given them the courage to divorce their husbands, something that moved but also troubled me.

In Mexico, I completed the translation of Lillian Hellman's book *Scoundrel Times* (*Tiempo de canallas*), published by Fondo de Cultura Económica Press in 1980. I also translated *Maybe*, another book of Lillian Hellman's. The Fondo Press contracted me to translate it but did not publish the translation. I still keep in my files a copy of this manuscript because I believe it is a better translation than the one that Fondo Press finally published.

My experience in Mexico was very important for me. Until then I thought I was a housewife and a mother, but I was hounded by the

Rosario Ferré with her three children, Luis, Rosaloren, and Benigno Trigo
at the Marbella house (ca. 1969)

question, what did it mean to be a writer? In Puerto Rico a writer was seen as a self-centered pretender unless he was a journalist or his work was useful to society. My first father-in-law used to say "Writers are always staring at their navels; they don't know what it means to earn a living by the sweat of their brow." For him, writers lived by sucking the blood out of those who worked. (This is still a fairly common point of view on the Island.) It was very different in Mexico. Writers were considered professionals. Writing was something everyone took seriously. They thought it was necessary to study and think about fiction, the life of the imagination. Commercial considerations, like whether the book would be a best seller or not, or if it would make money or not, were not part of the equation. The work of writing was well respected and to be a dedicated writer was widely recognized. Writing would not make you rich, but that was another reason for admiring writers.

Literature, like painting, is mysterious. The words and the colors may be the same, but the work of Picasso and the scrawls of a child are very different. The line that separates the work of art from an ordinary composition is momentary and hard to define. A secret mystery lies in its delicate and slippery nature. This is not always the case. Painters like Diego Rivera or David Alfaro Siqueiros, for example, have an impact on you from the very beginning. One recognizes their genius right away. But the work of more subtle artists like Leonora Carrington needs the passage of time before its quality rises to the surface. All these things became very clear to me during my stay in Mexico.

I rented a house in Coyoacán, a neighborhood that was popular with artists and writers, which was very stimulating, but I also began having difficulties in Mexico. The house was beautiful and belonged to Anita Villaurrutia, daughter of the famous Mexican composer Xavier Villaurrutia. There was a wall around the house 20 feet high, crowned with barbed wire and broken glass, and across the street from the house there was a *pulquería* with a sign that said "No women or dogs allowed." The neighborhood was old and quaint, but I had moved there

Luis A. Ferré among the public during the book launch of Fábulas de la garza desangrada at La Tertulia bookstore

with my three children, and life for them was extremely complicated. They had to ride two buses to get to the Colegio Madrid, getting up at five in the morning to arrive by eight. Several times men tried to harass my daughter, and she had to get off the bus in a hurry with her two brothers running behind her to catch the next bus. Another time I was robbed at knife-point on the bus; after that I always took a taxi.

Life in Mexico City was very difficult due to the contaminated air and to the 13 million people that lived there (today the population is 20 million, almost twice the amount). Water was a monumental problem and I contracted salmonella five times, leading my gastroenterologist, a German specialist, to warn me that I risked chronic illness if I did not return to Puerto Rico.

But overall, the experience of living in Mexico was dear to me. I met many writers, marvelous people like Elena Poniatowska, Antonio Alatorre, José Emilio Pacheco, and many more, whom I have regarded as my friends throughout the years. My first contact with the intellectual scene of Mexico was one afternoon when I visited the Centro de Escritores Mexicanos, where groups would meet under the guidance of the writer Salvador Elizondo. That afternoon I met the poet David Huerta, the novelist Héctor Manjarréz, Paloma Villegas, Elsa Cross, and other Mexican writers.

Even though intellectual life in Mexico was enormously stimulating, living with Jorge was difficult from the beginning. I discovered that Mexicans were a self-absorbed people with a sense of humor and a sense of life that was very different from that of Puerto Ricans. I was troubled by the fact that no one laughed at my jokes, and I did not think that theirs were very funny either.

During my stay in Mexico I wrote *El árbol y sus sombras*, a collection of essays on literary topics published by the Fondo de Cultura Económica in 1989. I included essays about my favorite authors, like Sor Juana Inés de la Cruz, Tina Modotti, Galdós, Vallejo, Sarduy, and others. I returned to Puerto Rico with my children in 1976, and Jorge, who had originally thought about staying in Mexico, returned with us to the Island. He lived here three years but never adapted.

Once we returned to San Juan, I began to write the book of poetry *Fábulas de la garza desangrada*, published by Joaquín Mortiz in 1982 in the collection *Las Dos Orillas*. The book was launched at La Tertulia bookstore in Río Piedras, and Father was there. I chose the title from

Tales of Gengi, a book by a Chinese courtesan from the 13th century. I wrote it almost in one sitting, on a yellow legal pad and pencil. I was never able to write poetry directly on a typewriter because the noise of the keys disturbs the bond between feeling and paper. Silence is necessary for poetry, and machines can choke the flow of ideas.

From the very beginning, *Fábulas de la garza desangrada* was related to the book of feminist essays *Sitio a Eros*. In those essays I studied the lives of women who seemed admirable to me because of the courage of their struggle to succeed in life. Most of them were artists, and they were all brave; and for that reason, I dedicated the book to my daughter with the epigraph, "to her fierce hope."

In *Fábulas de la garza desangrada* I focused on the life of a number of mythical women from classical legend: Shakespeare's Ophelia, Cervantes's Dorotea, Daphne, Antigone, Ariadne, and others. But I gave their lives a very different ending. Ophelia assassinates Othello by dropping a poisoned pearl in his wine goblet. Dorotea celebrates her triumphant victory over her rapist, Don Fernando. Daphne gets rid of Apollo without having to turn into a tree. The poem "Fábula de la garza desangrada" is a counterpoint to the poem "Piedra de sol" written by Octavio Paz. The idea of "Piedra de sol," that woman could be fulfilled only by sacrificing herself at the altar of love, seemed absurd to me, a fetish of Latin American machismo that owed much to Aztec sacrifices.

I was very happy with the overall tone of *Fábulas*. The book was launched at La Tertulia, but I didn't tell my father about it because many of the poems were erotic. But he saw the ad in the paper and came on his own. He sat down in the front row, and from then on he always went to all my book launches in Puerto Rico.

It took me four years to write the novel *Maldito amor*. Just like *Papeles de Pandora* and *Sitio a Eros*, I wrote it on my second portable typewriter, a Smith Corona. I gave that machine a real beating. I traveled everywhere with it, and one time during a visit to New York with Jorge, I locked myself in the hotel and did not come out until I finished the story "Maquinolandera." The story received an honorable mention in the Ateneo competition that year. It took me three years to write the stories from *Papeles de Pandora*. I always was a slow writer, more a reviser than a writer; each story took me up to 18 drafts. When the book was finished, I had it memorized from start to finish. Later when I wrote my longer novels, I used countless reams of paper on the computer. It would give me nightmares just thinking about the trees I destroyed with each print out.

I learned the first secret to becoming a writer at the H. Perry secretarial school in Ponce. There I discovered that it was easy for me to typewrite and I soon became the fastest student in the class. This surely had something to do with the fact that my parents made me practice the piano every day, but I was always bored despite my love of music. My calligraphy was deplorable and often I could not understand what I had written. In learning to typewrite I finally understood what I wrote. My mother had a lot to do with all of this, since it was she who forced me to change from being left-handed to right-handed. I was born left-handed, but she insisted that when left-handed people sat at the table to eat, they always bumped elbows with their neighbor on the left, which made them spill their soup. Therefore my love for writing had a hint of revolt against convention from the very beginning, and this left its mark on me forever. Writing using both hands at a typewriter fixes the problem of identity, whether one is left-handed or right-handed. From that moment on, I became ambidextrous, and I've always been able to write with both hands in pencil or pen.

The typewriter is a filter between thought and the page that allows us to give form to our ideas. When writing by hand, nothing stands between us and the flow of ideas, and if our thoughts are in disarray, so is our writing. When I was young, my thoughts were in a state of confusion. The typewriter helped me to clarify them. Ultimately an impersonal and disciplined machine, the type came out neat and clear on the page. One would think another person was doing the writing. The typewriter offers a useful and healthy distance when we write with the imagination or with the emotions; in other words, when we write fiction.

Some years later I discovered that writing on a computer created an even greater distance, and this realization made writing even easier for me. But I always had a love-hate relationship with the computer. The computer is what Góngora said about Lope de Vega: "A noble steed, but unrestrained." When the computer decides to bolt, no one in Christendom can stop it. At times it breaks away and overtakes the thought process itself; at other times it prefers to erase ideas. On many occasions I lost complete manuscripts by hitting the wrong key, and every time I faced such impossible situations I felt like throwing the computer out the window. Writing on a typewriter was a totally different experience from writing on a computer. It was easier in the sense that my thoughts were not trapped inside a plastic box; they were free. But I was a slave to scissors and tape, and my manuscripts would become as long as medieval scrolls, which I rolled to keep all the fragments together. The typewriter was totally dependable, it never broke down, and it never threatened to erase the text at the slightest brush with a tragic key, but the computer was the future, and I continued to use it. I usually write directly on the computer without setting my thoughts on paper first, as if I were playing the piano. Writing gives me great satisfaction, and during those moments when it is impossible to write and I walk past the computer, I look at it with nostalgia and I can see a little cloud of happiness hanging over the keyboard, waiting for me to return.

Mortiz published *Maldito amor* in 1986, and I went to Mexico for the book launch, which was organized by Elena Poniatowska and Margot Glanz at the Universidad Autónoma de México (UNAM). It was my first attempt at writing a novel, but I had neither the stamina nor the writing experience to write a long one. *Maldito amor* is a short novel with three stories interconnected by characters who all belong to the same family. I used the structure of the Japanese film *Rashomon*, where the same story is told by four characters from different points of view. All the versions cancel each other out like a row of dominoes falling on each other. The title, *Maldito amor*, is also ambiguous; it is simultaneously the love of the Puerto Rican countryside, and the love between a man and a woman, two beings who are enemies from the very beginning.

In 1979, Professor Ángel Rama, who had initially been my master's thesis director in the UPR, lived with his wife, Marta Traba, in the United States. He and his wife arrived in Puerto Rico in 1969. They were a truly intellectual couple that added much to the quality of education in UPR. Ángel was a Uruguayan literary critic of much renown. His classes on the theory of the novel and on Felisberto Hernández filled to capacity. Marta taught art appreciation and art history, and her classes were also very popular. In 1972, the State Department office in San Juan refused to renew their visa, and they had to leave Puerto Rico. After living and working in various countries, Ángel was offered a pres-

Rosario Ferré and Ángel Rama in Maryland

tigious teaching position at the University of Maryland. Both moved to Washington, D.C. in 1979. Once there, Ángel offered a position to Jorge. He felt wretched in Puerto Rico and accepted the offer. In 1980, we moved to College Park, the home of the University of Maryland.

While living in College Park, I translated *Maldito amor* to English, and Ballantine Press published it in 1980. Gregory Rabassa had translated one of my stories from *Papeles de Pandora* and published it in the prestigious American journal *The Kenyon Review*. Rabassa's translation was my letter of introduction to Ballantine and they were interested in *Maldito amor*. This was a miracle since publishing houses in the U.S. never accept book manuscripts without the backing of a literary agent, but this was a barrier I set out to break. The title itself was untrans-

Agustín Costa, Rosario Ferré, José F. Santiago, and Wolfgang Binder during the launch of Maldito Amor (Kristallzucker) in Germany, 1991

latable so I called it *Sweet Diamond Dust*, the brand of sugar produced by the De la Valle family. (*Maldito amor* means both "Damned Love" and "Doomed Love" but it doesn't mean either one exactly.) In 1992 the novel received the *Liberatur Prix* at the Frankfort Book Fair. Wolfgang Binder translated the novel to German as *Kristallzucker*, and it was published by Rotpunkverlag Press in 1991.[2]

Wolfgang Binder, professor from Erlangen University, translated the book of fantastic short stories *El medio pollito* into German with the title *Das halbe Hühnchen auf dem Web zum Palast* for Verlag der Ev.-Luth. Mission Erlangen Press in 1990. The book launch was in Munich and was quite successful, since Germans seem to enjoy that kind of story. *El medio pollito* in German was important for me because it was the first of my books to cross the Atlantic and to be published in Europe, something that had been my goal from the beginning. I wanted to break the publication barrier, the confinement to Puerto Rico or to the United States. I owe this accomplishment to Wolfgang, to his flawless translations and to his contacts in the publishing world. In Germany they changed the title of the novel *Vecindarios excéntricos* to *Die Stimmen der*

*Rosario Ferré with Wolfgang Binder at the
book launch of Maldito amor*

Träume, (The River of Dreams). Elisabeth Müeller was in charge of the
translation, published by Krüger Verlag Press in 1999.

Later, *Maldito amor* was published in Italy by EO Press with the
title *Maledetto amore*. They changed my name to Josefina Ferré, because
Josefina is my middle name, and because my first name, Rosario, ends
in "o" and there are no feminine names in Italian that end in that
vowel. The book launch was in Turin at the ceremony for the *Grinzane
Cavour* prize. Agustín Costa and I went there with a group of Puerto
Ricans: Ana Lydia Vega, Pedro Pietri, and Antonio "Toño" Martorell,
all of whom had books published in Italian. The Nobel laureate in
literature Derek Walcott and other European authors were also
present. Pedro Pietri arrived dressed in black and carrying a black
leather suitcase. He delivered his poems and suddenly opened his
suitcase and threw hundreds of little packets of prophylactics at the
audience. The Italians were in shock, but they could see the value of
his *Puerto Rican Obituary*.

I had translated some of the short stories in *Papeles de Pandora*
into English with Diana Velez, and it surprised me how much the text
changed in translation. It was almost like writing a different book, and
the process intrigued me. One became a different person in each language and saw the world in a different way. The translation of *Maldito
amor* was easy for me, and it only took me three months to complete
it. The book was well received, and in future I decided to continue
translating my own texts.

I was at the University of Maryland from 1981 until 1985. I wanted to earn a doctorate, but before admission to the graduate program in the Spanish Department at the University of Maryland, I first had to finish my master's degree at UPR. I traveled to Puerto Rico to meet with José Ramón de la Torre, who was the director of Hispanic Studies at that time, and presented my case to him. It had been nine years since I had left the university, and after ten years the courses were no longer valid. I had one year to write my thesis, and my thesis director Ángel Rama was already dead. I had to look for another director and asked several friends in the department to take me on, but nobody had the time. José Ramón recommended that I speak with Professor Federico Acevedo to see if he was willing to do it, and he graciously accepted. I returned to Maryland and locked myself in our College Park apartment, which was part of a lower middle-class residential complex, to write my master's thesis. I would send the chapters to Federico Acevedo by mail. The thesis was about Felisberto Hernández, a Uruguayan author who wrote fantastic short stories, and I wrote it in one year. My confinement was so extreme that some Hindu neighbors we had in the building approached me and asked whether I would be interested in babysitting their children, since I was always locked up at home not doing anything. I thanked them for their offer, but naturally I declined.

After my thesis was approved with honors by UPR, I was admitted to the doctoral program at the University of Maryland, where Jorge was teaching. It was a very good department. Juan Ramón Jiménez had taught there many years before. They had professors from Mexico and Argentina, among them Tomás Eloy Martínez, Ariel Gutiérrez, José Emilio Pacheco, and Antonio Alatorre. Ángel Rama, who was responsible for our move to Maryland, died shortly after our arrival in a tragic Iberia plane crash. A new aircraft of Swedish design crashed after takeoff from Barajas Airport in Madrid, killing all the passengers. I was counting on him for help in Maryland, but I had to write the thesis on Felisberto all by myself. Some years later I rewrote the thesis and published it as a book with the title *Felisberto Hernández, acomodador de realidades fantásticas*. Siglo XXI Press published it in Mexico in 1986.

That was the first time I used a computer. It was a soft green Mac, an ordinary two by two box, back when they were all the same. It was a bitter struggle to liberate my thoughts from the machine. Its plastic walls surrounded my mind and they held my ideas prisoner. Writing did not flow on the screen. Later, I realized that I needed to print out the text and see it take form on the page. Before that, sentences were no more than impulses; they didn't really exist, and it was difficult to develop them. Also, it was important to see what came before and after the text, all of which remained outside the viewing screen. Reading a book makes for a lateral vision that allows you to see what comes before and after. But on the computer thoughts fall into an abyss on both sides of the screen. After several trials, I was able to break through the electronic barrier and I conquered the computer, but it all depended on reading the text after it was printed on the page.

Once I finished my doctoral courses in Maryland, I had to write the dissertation I had proposed on Julio Cortázar's eight books of short stories. The title was *La filiación romántica en los cuentos de Julio Cortázar*. My dissertation director was Saúl Sosnowsky, who was then the department chair. Later, in 1991, Editorial Cultural Press published the dissertation as a book with the title *Cortázar: el romántico en su observatorio*.

During those years, I taught a course on Julio Cortázar at Berkeley, and two courses, one on Latin American women's poetry and the other on the fantastic short story in Latin America, at Johns Hopkins— later, in 1990, I taught these two courses at the University of Puerto Rico, in the Comparative Literature Department. In 1984, I taught a course on Puerto Rican literature at Rutgers University, New Jersey campus. I always liked to teach but found it time consuming and I decided to dedicate myself to writing.

Jorge was still uncertain whether to live in Mexico or in the United States and he went to Mexico for six months, renting an apartment in Mexico City. When he returned, he went to live in College Park, and did not want to move to Washington, D.C., where I had purchased a small apartment on Q Street at 17th. We began to live separately and finally decided to divorce. This meant that I had to write my dissertation on Cortázar while living alone in Washington in rather difficult circumstances. I wrote my dissertation in a year and a half and was awarded honors after my defense. At last, I got my diploma and never returned to the University of Maryland.

From that moment on, I made a completely different life for myself in Washington, D.C., meeting people and making friends from the Organization of American States, Georgetown University, American

University, from the embassies, and from other cultural centers. Washington is a wonderful city with parks filled with flowers, and I thought it was my garden. My apartment was a small walk-up with two bedrooms where I lived happily for six years.

In 1989, I met Agustín Costa, a Puerto Rican architect who had lived in the U.S. for 24 years. His office was in Reston, Virginia. We began to date and eventually moved to a beautiful house at 2126 Leroy Place in Washington. Agustín has been my partner during the last 24 years, and has always given me his support during the good and the bad times of my life.

Rosario Ferré with her husband, Agustín Costa

*Agustín Costa, Rosario Ferré, Kelly Oliver, Benigno Trigo, and Luis Trigo
at the Plaza Hotel, New York, during the Christmas season, 1999*

The Ferré-Costa family

In 1991 we returned together to Puerto Rico from Washington and were married in a civil ceremony with Antonio Andreu serving as judge. We were married at my father's house in San Patricio and a few friends came to celebrate with us. My aunt Isolina was the minister who gave us her blessing. Agustín and I went to live in my house on Marbella Street, which was the same as before, and we only had to do a minor renovation. Agustín was able to set up his office in a building that used to house the old garages in the back.

I wrote *El coloquio de las perras* shortly after I returned to Puerto Rico. Editorial Cultural Press published it in 1991, and we launched the book at Hermes bookstore on Ashford Avenue when my niece María Luisa Ferré Rangel owned it. We had a lovely reception attended by all of my nieces and nephews. *Coloquio* is a book of feminist essays of literary criticism that parodies Miguel de Cervantes's *El coloquio de los perros* and it is dedicated to Ani Fernández, professor at UPR, and Jean Franco, professor at Columbia University. This is the book I've had the most fun with; I laughed out loud as I wrote it. The essay is a critical review of the Latin American Boom writers whose female characters always play secondary roles, as is the case with Mario Vargas Llosa. The antifeminist prejudice is hidden but still present in all the Boom writers, and it surprised me that no one had pointed this out.

The essay followed two stray bitches named Franca and Fina (cousins of Berganza and Cipión) as they took a walk on the grounds of the old Spanish fortress, El Morro, while discussing the works of José Donoso, Jorge Luis Borges, Carlos Fuentes, and others. They pointed out their angry prejudice against women. The cover had a picture of two little bitches climbing stairs in Old San Juan. Unfortunately the title was misunderstood by many, especially by the average reader. I remember a day when I was seated at Howard Johnson's (across the street from Hermes bookstore) drinking a milk shake when the waitress asked me to sign her copy of the book. "You don't know how happy I am that you wrote it. It was about time somebody wrote a book about Puerto Rico's cute mutts," she said to me. I didn't say anything and I signed her book, but with a heavy conscience.

My second book of poetry, *Las dos Venecias*, was published by Editorial Joaquín Mortiz Press in 1992. It was a celebration of femininity and at the same time a search for the mother's body. In the book I compared the feminine body to the city of Venice, filled with waterways and secret passages. We launched the book in Mexico, and it was the last time I saw don Joaquín Díez-Canedo, who had so generously published all my books up to that time. He died shortly after that, and I always felt guilty for not having thanked him publicly, since I was a Puerto Rican writer, unknown in Mexico. Don Joaquín was an extraordinary person. He arrived in Mexico escaping the Spanish Civil War and invested all his money and that of his wife in Mortiz Press. He often published young, unknown authors whom he liked. He had an exquisite taste but did not make enough money to survive. They were unusual, distinctive, and Avant Garde writers whom nobody knew at the start. In the end he sold the business to Planeta, which immediately made the press profitable but stopped publishing unknown yet excellent writers.

In 1992, I also published *Memorias de Ponce: Biografía de Don Luis A. Ferré*, which I wrote together with my father. Editorial Norma Press of Puerto Rico published the book and it was launched at the Arsenal in Old San Juan. Members of my family read aloud from the book; my father, my aunt Isolina Ferré, my nephew Luis Alberto, and my niece María Luisa Ferré Rangel all read fragments from it. Unfortunately my children were not in Puerto Rico and could not participate.

In 1994, I published the novel *La batalla de las vírgenes*, at Editorial Universitaria Press. This is a satirical novel about the cults to the Virgen Del Pozo and the Virgen De Medjugorje, but many people didn't think it was funny and took it seriously instead; Carmen Dolores Hernández published a devastating review in *El Nuevo Día* criticizing me for making fun of topics that were sacred (supposedly) even though the scenes were patently absurd. I spoke with Father Fernando Picó and told him what had happened. I sent him a copy of the book and asked him to read it to see what he thought. He was kind enough to write a review in the *San Juan Star* defending the book and pointing out its real subject: the injustice of class difference within the Church.

I began writing *La casa de la laguna* when I just arrived in Puerto Rico in 1992. I am sure that I would not have been able to write it if I had not lived in the United States for the previous eight years. This temporal distance allowed me to see more clearly the reality of my own country, and to work with issues that were both emotionally charged, and also too close to me. But, if I had stayed in the United States, I would not have been able to write it either; in other words,

I had to return to the Island to write the novel. When you return to your place of origin after a long period of time, you bring back the life you left behind, projecting it onto the life you now lead. It is a constant double exposure; you live simultaneously in the present and the past. Everybody goes through this, but this is a rich experience for the artist because of the issues it raises in us. It is also a source of inspiration that helps us know ourselves better. We are two at the same time: the person that we took with us when we left, and the person we found when we returned.

I wrote the first version of *La casa de la laguna* in Spanish. I was helped by the fact that the course on the Techniques of the Novel I had taken at the UPR with Mario Vargas Llosa was still fresh in my mind, and also by the fact that the class had been so valuable to me. The structure was very complicated, and I had to put the chapters on the floor, around my bed, so that I could look at them and find the way out of its labyrinth. At night Agustín had to jump over the chapters in the dark so that he could go to the bathroom, and I had to do the same. The process took about a year.

I was pleased when I finished writing it. Form and content, theme and structure, history and fiction all came together in the title. *La casa de la laguna* was *La casa de la laguna*: in other words, it was impossible to separate the architecture of the figurative house from the themes of the book. The house on the lagoon is located on a swamp, and for that reason it is amphibious ground, land and water at the same time. Puerto Rico is similarly located on a swamp of politically unstable and treacherous terrain, where we all move. The novel confirms the fact that history and fiction are but two sides of the same coin; both are necessary for knowledge.

Language is one of the important themes of the novel. Isabel Monfort becomes a person (as well as a character) through language. She asserts her version of events (and her truth) over her husband's, Quintín Mendizábal, who is a historian. I tried to say many things in that novel, for example, that there is no single truth but many, and that women and men speak different languages. In a sense, this is the reason why I became a writer: nobody has a monopoly on the truth, and this is essential to my thinking about what it means to be a society that lives a life of freedom.

Since publishing *Zona. Carga y descarga*, literature has been for me an Avant Garde proposition that is valid still. The allegorical destruction (*carga*) and creation (*descarga*) of cultural and social spaces that took place in its pages captured the drama of a new postmodern identity. A vision of a Puerto Rico that was no longer logocentric and homogeneous, that went beyond the principles of nationalism but did not deny access to them, was knocking at the door. Nationalism was still very important for the sense of identity, but it was only one voice added to a diverse choir universally expressed. This is why I believe that *La casa de la laguna* is my most accomplished novel, the one that contains my deepest insights.

After I finished the novel, I didn't want to send it to a local or to a Latin American press. I had published three works of fiction already, but my books still did not reach beyond the Latin American and Puerto Rican context. They were published in Mexico thanks to my friendship with don Joaquín. But my ambition was to be published in Spain, and maybe even in Europe. It occurred to me that a more effective strategy would be to publish the book first in English; that way, it would come out as an original work. I thought that the distribution system of the book industry would give the novel much more exposure if it was published in the U.S. market.

I had experience as a translator; I had done the English translation for *Maldito amor* and thought that translating a two-hundred-page manuscript was not an impossible task. I sent it (still in Spanish) to Susan Bergholz, a New York literary agent recommended by Tomás Colchie, himself the agent for the majority of Latin American writers in the U.S. at the time. Susan in turn represented a considerable number of Latina writers, for the most part Mexican-Americans who were very popular, like Denise Chávez, Sandra Cisneros, Ana Castillo, and Julia Álvarez (Dominican). Although Susan did not speak Spanish, she advised me to send the manuscript to Farrar, Straus, and Giroux to see if they were interested. If Farrar Straus accepted the book, she would agree to become my agent and represent me.

Nobody in Farrar, Straus, and Giroux read or spoke Spanish, but they liked the plot summary I sent them and they looked for a little old Persian man, who promised to meet me in New York. He arrived at the Madison hotel wearing a black overcoat and a Russian hat of astrakhan fur, and I gave him the manuscript as if it were made of gold. He assured me he read Spanish and that he would study it with care. Later

I realized that American publishers were so prejudiced against Latin American writers that they only trusted American, European, and, if necessary, Persian readers to review their texts.

My Persian friend loved the novel and recommended it to Farrar, Straus, and Giroux. The press decided to publish the manuscript and asked me to translate it. I agreed to do the translation, but it was separate from our business deal and they would pay me nothing for it. Translators were too expensive, and it would have been impossible to translate a two-hundred-page novel by an unknown Puerto Rican author. I agreed to the terms set by Farrar, Straus, and Giroux, and they paid me an advance of $25,000, which was more than I had earned from any of my previous books. John Glussman, who was considered royalty by the editorial houses, would be my editor.

Susan called me, and I signed a contract with her agreeing that she would be my agent, although it bothered me that she insisted on being my agent in the world of Hispanic literature. She did not speak one word of Spanish, and I could represent myself perfectly well, as I had done up till then with *Papeles de Pandora* and *Maldito amor*. But Susan was relentless and it was impossible to make her change her mind: either she was my universal agent or there was no deal. Nevertheless, she was very effective disseminating my novels and successfully negotiated contracts with more than twenty different countries that translated my books: Taiwan, China, France, Japan, Italy, Greece, Poland, and the Netherlands, among others. She was completely dedicated to her writers and this was very beneficial for me. I owe her a great deal and will always be grateful. Susan was a good friend.

I began the English version of *La casa de la laguna* when I returned home to Marbella; it took me two years to finish it. The translated novel doubled in size and grew to 400 pages long. John Glussman was the editor. He also edited *Eccentric Neighborhoods* and *Flight of the Swan*, both published some years later.

The House on the Lagoon was nominated for the National Book Award in August of 1995, an honor I did not expect. Agustín and I went to the banquet in New York where they announced the winners of the prizes. It was a night full of emotion. Our table was in front of the display where the prizes were sitting in a row, plaques made of glass with the names of the winners engraved on them. Since I had 20-20 vision, though the letters were inverted I could read the words on the award that corresponded to me, and I saw that it was engraved with the name of Philip Roth, a well known American writer. Needless to say, when we came close to the moment when the name of the winner was read out loud, I was crying, and Agustín did not know why.

The House on the Lagoon was an unusual success. It sold almost 100,000 copies in the United States, and thanks to its success it was translated into French, Italian, Greek, Dutch, and German. The Germans changed the title without consulting me and titled the book *Isabel*. It was published by Scherz Verlag Press in 1997. I think they did it to benefit from the popularity of Isabel Allende in Germany at the time. The final translation (into Spanish) of *La casa de la laguna* was 500 pages long. I discovered that to say the same thing in Spanish took more words, and the novel had grown so much from its original version in Spanish, that I had to translate it again. Several editions were published in Spanish: by Emecé Press in Spain and Argentina and by Vintage Español in New York.

The book launch for *La casa de la laguna* took place in a property owned by Israel Rodríguez & Partners, located on Ponce de León Avenue next to the Excelsior Hotel. The property is a house designed by the architect Nechodoma and is very similar to the house of my novel, also located behind the lagoon. Florita and Israel kindly put at my disposal the house where their advertising firm was located, and made a beautiful poster with a picture of the Condado lagoon in the background. Mayra Montero did the introduction and many friends celebrated with us that night. The book tour for *La casa de la laguna* was my first in the United States. The publishers sent me to Los Angeles, San Francisco, Houston, Pittsburgh, and several other cities to promote the book. Often Puerto Ricans came to the city bookstores to meet me and to tell me how much they had enjoyed the novel, and that they were glad to read about Puerto Rico in English because they had lost their Spanish and felt disconnected from their homeland. I always went alone on those tours, but when they sent me to Europe Agustín came with me. Together we went to Paris, Frankfurt, Amsterdam, and Munich, where I gave lectures and granted interviews. In Munich, I made a mistake about the time of the interview with *Der Spiegel*, and I missed an important opportunity to promote the novel.

I began to write *Vecindarios excéntricos* in 1996, and by 1997 I had a Spanish version that I submitted to Marta Aponte Alsina at Editorial de la Universidad de Puerto Rico Press. They wanted to publish it, but I backed out and chose instead to do what I had done with *La casa de la laguna* to get greater distribution. I put away the original Spanish manuscript, and I began to write the text in English; to my surprise it became a completely different novel.

The characters reached a depth they did not originally have. The first version was more autobiographical, and though cannibalized, it is still a different book that is not published yet.

Farrar, Straus, and Giroux published *Vecindarios excéntricos* as *Eccentric Neighborhoods* in 1998. This book is about the Puerto Rico that one finds on the West of the Island, just like *La casa de la laguna* describes the North and the South. It is similar in structure to *A Thousand and One Nights*: a series of related stories strung together like a strand of pearls. The character Elvira is a girl in search of her mother, and all of her aunts offer her different approaches to follow. Finally, she finds her own approach, which is that of the writer.

Vecindarios excéntricos also sold well in the United States. Exactly as happened with *La casa de la laguna*, *The New York Times Book Review* published a positive review of the novel, and it was translated into German, Dutch, Russian, Japanese, Italian, Taiwanese, and Greek. The Spanish version grew by more than one hundred pages, just like *La casa de la laguna*. The book launch in Puerto Rico was in Cronopios bookstore; it had the participation of Axel Anderson and Eneid Routté, two marvelous human beings.

My next novel was *Flight of the Swan*, published in 2001 by Farrar, Straus, and Giroux. Edgardo Rodríguez Juliá wrote a beautiful essay about the book and he launched it at the Raúl Juliá Theater of the Museo de Arte de Puerto Rico. Rebeca Canchani of the Ballet Concierto danced "The Dying Swan" by Saint-Saens, and Idalia Pérez Garay (an artist and poetry lover whom I admire) dramatized the novel. Later, there was another book launch at the Museo de Arte de Ponce.

For the first time, I tried to write the book in English from the very beginning, thinking I would save myself the trouble of translating from English to Spanish, but it did not happen that way. I wrote directly in English only with great difficulty, and the words did not flow. I don't know exactly why, but a story flows directly from its language in some mysterious way. When I begin to write, what I have in mind is more like the seed of a story, a brief anecdote that later expands with each rewriting. It was like this in the process of writing all of my works. Yet again, I found that fiction has nothing to do with life, and has everything to do with it.

The story told in the novel was real: Anna Pavlova visited Puerto Rico in 1914, when United States citizenship was granted to Puerto Ricans. She was *en tournée* in Cuba and on the way there stopped in Puerto Rico with her dance troupe. Pavlova disembarked in San Juan planning on a short visit, but the Bolshevik coup in her country surprised her here. As a result, she was left without a passport and neither she nor her troupe could continue the trip. It was necessary to send her agent to New York to conduct the business to get new passports so that they could leave, but this took more than three months. During that time Pavlova was forced to stay in Puerto Rico and she toured the Island performing in Arecibo, Mayagüez, and Ponce. That was all I knew about what happened, but I went to the University of Puerto Rico library and there I found a photograph from Pavlova's visit to the Island, and a number of articles with pictures about her in the 1914 issue of *El Puerto Rico ilustrado*. For me, the most important find

Enrique García, Pilar Reguero, Agustín Costa, Myrna Báez, and Rosario Ferré

Myrna Báez, Rosario Ferré, and Pilar Reguer

was a photo that showed Pavlova holding two bird cages in her hand, pets that went with her everywhere. From there, I slowly developed the story, which is completely made up: the romance with the Puerto Rican guerilla who is locked in a struggle with the federal authorities over the issue of citizenship.

All of the books I wrote after this were collections of essays and poetry: in 1995, Editorial Cultural Press published my *Antología personal*, which included poems from 1976 to 1994, but the book had so many mistakes that I asked Francisco Vázquez to withdraw it from the market. After this, Vintage Español in New York published *Duelo del lenguaje/Language Duel*, a bilingual book of poetry. Alan West was responsible for the translations into English of some of its poems. José Félix Gómez launched it at Castle Books. Editorial Callejón Press published my latest book of poetry, *Fisuras*, in 2006.

A la sombra de tu nombre is a book of essays that Alfaguara Press published in 2000, and *Las puertas del placer*, another collection of essays, was also published by Alfaguara in 2005. Both had covers designed after works by Myrna Báez, the best Puerto Rican painter today, and my best friend.

At the beginning of the 1980s I wrote several children's stories based on *El conde Lucanor*. Through the years I had written other children's stories—*El medio pollito* (1978), *Los cuentos de Juan Bobo* (1981), and *La mona que le pisaron la cola* (1981), all published by Ediciones Huracán Press. I published these three books, together with the stories based on *El conde Lucanor*, in 1989 in a volume entitled *Sonatinas*, also with Huracán. Later between 1996 and 1997, Alfaguara Press published them separately. I love writing for children; that kind of story is similar to poetry: its symbolism is almost transparent and it can be easily associated with everyday life, and with what seems to be ordinary, because it is so close to us. I am interested still in publishing in this genre.

I still need to talk about a novel that I published with Alfaguara in 2009 with the title *Lazos de sangre*. While I was writing it, I kept thinking about the book *Lazos de familia* by Clarice Lispector. Just as in Brazilian families, innocence and betrayal often go hand in hand in extended Puerto Rican families and they are difficult to separate. We passionately love those we betray as if betrayal was unquestionable proof of our faithfulness. Families are like nets in a stormy sea where we are both caught and supported. In *Lazos de sangre*, the cousins, Rose, Irene, Angela, and Julia are endlessly conspiring against each other but they also feel a basic, unbreakable, and tender bond that makes them love each other beyond betrayal and death.

NOTES

1. The journal's history is documented in Lucila Ramos's excellent dissertation and in an essay I presented at a conference in recognition of my work held at the Mayagüez campus of the University of Puerto Rico and at the Museum of Contemporary Art in 2005.

2. José Fernando Santiago Morales was in charge of the cover design for *Kristallzucker*. He made a collage of photos from his parents' wedding and a piece of cloth belonging to his grandmother.

*Enrique Laguerre and Rosario Ferré during a celebration
of Enrique Laguerre at La Fortaleza*

Epilogue

This is an account of how I wrote my books. I dedicated a lot of time to writing, time that perhaps I should have dedicated to love, to my children, to my husband, to my friends, or simply to living. I was very lucky to find editors who supported me, and writing companions who helped me correct and improve my manuscripts as much as possible. Ángel Rama was among the people that inspired me most. He was very special to me because he made me realize that writing was my vocation. For Ángel, writing was a sacred duty. The talents we receive at birth are gifts from God, and not cultivating them is a betrayal. From Mario Vargas Llosa, I learned the technical complexities that are inherent to the Latin American novel. He was also an inspiration and a great help. From Doña Margot Arce, I learned to love Hispanic literature, Garcilaso de la Vega, Góngora, and Cervantes; and also from Arcadio Díaz Quiñones, Enrique Laguerre, and Luce López-Baralt. Carmen Dolores Hernández's work as a critic of Puerto Rican literature has been monumental. The breadth of her knowledge and her intelligence place her well above the rest of the critics of our time. Carmen Dolores analyzed all my texts, and even though we did not always agree, her insights were very helpful and always constructive. Unfortunately she has not been properly recognized for her important work.

The Peruvian writer and literary critic Julio Ortega has been an essential source of support, and an advocate of Puerto Rican literature for many years. He nominated me for the honorary degree of Doctor of Humanities that I received on April 28, 1997 from Vartan Gregori-

Nilita Vientós Gastón and Rosario Ferré

an, the President of Brown University. I shared that distinction with Carlos Fuentes, Víctor García de la Concha (Secretary to the Royal Academy of the Spanish Language), and Jesús de Polanco (president of the Prisa Group and founder of the newspaper *El País*). It was a special ceremony dedicated to the Department of Hispanic Studies at Brown and part of the Spanish Language Day celebrations. Carlos Fuentes gave the acceptance speech in the name of all the honorees.

I met Julio Ortega at the International Congress of Contemporary Literature of the Americas: The Writer and His World, organized by the Interamerican University of Puerto Rico, which took place February 24 to 26, 1982. Juan Rulfo and Jorge Amado attended the conference. From that moment on, Julio and I corresponded. On one of his visits to Puerto Rico he interviewed me, and later the interview appeared in *Reapropiaciones*, published by the Editorial de la Universidad de Puerto Rico Press. He also included me in a marvelous book entitled *La Cervantiada*, published in 1995, which collected texts from various writers about Cervantes. There I published my poem "Óbolo a Dorotea," which Carlos Fuentes liked very much. The poem was first published in *Fábulas de la garza desangrada*.

On December 19, 2007, I was named honorary member of the Puerto Rican Academy of the Spanish Language together with Julio Ortega, for which I am profoundly grateful. To share such an honor with him was an even greater distinction.

I have always been supported by my children, Rosaloren, Beni, and Luisito, and by my husband, Agustín Costa, with whom I've shared much of the adventure of my life, a man of a generosity beyond compare. The greatest compensation for my work has not been any certificate or trophy, but the satisfaction that writing gave me, and the happiness I felt during the process.

Literature today is threatened by many things. On a world-wide level it is often banal and superficial, perhaps because of the jumble of universal cultures. We are not sure of who we are, or of the way we are, and we live in a shifting borderland of countless languages and identities. We often find ourselves floating, adrift in a sea of flotsam, as my son Benigno Trigo points out in one of his essays on literature: today "Borders and Barnes & Noble are full of authors, the internet is full of blogs, and writing is so easy that it is even disposable." In such

Julio Ortega delivers a speech after his induction into the Puerto Rican Academy of the Spanish Language, December 19, 2007

Carmen Dolores Hernández during the nomination of Rosario Ferré as an honorary member of the Puerto Rican Academy of the Spanish Language, December 19, 2007

Luce López-Baralt reading Rosario Ferré's speech of induction to the Puerto Rican Academy of the Spanish Language; in the background Eduardo Forastieri and José Luis Vega, December 19, 2007

a setting, it might be difficult to evaluate contemporary literature, but we must still hope that our effort and our dedication to literature are not in vain.

"The word became flesh and lived among us" is the beginning of the Gospel according to Saint John. Verbs are forms of action and both are forms of energy. In his *Essay on the Origin of Languages,* Jean Jacques Rousseau says that language is proper to man because his passionate origins are in language: "We could say that needs dictated the first gestures, and passions tore out our first voices." In this sense, I have been very fortunate because writing has always been my labor and my passion.

To write is a gift of prophesy; it is always to rewrite, to discover something that was already written. It is like dusting off a very old text that came before us in time. In that sense, to write is hard but consoling labor. When you finish a well-written text, you know, without a doubt, it had to be that way.

On Entering the Academy

This tongue that holds my soul
reached me from afar burdened with honors
profound meanings
like the bones that hold my body

— **"This tongue that holds my soul," FISURAS, 2006** —

To be inducted as an honorary member of the Puerto Rican Academy of the Spanish Language is a distinction for which I am profoundly grateful.[1] More than a civic duty, it is the recognition of the fulfillment of a spiritual duty. Language is like our blood; it nourishes our being and makes us human. Unamuno says that language is the "blood" of the people. It defines and describes; it sets limits and norms of propriety and conduct. The battle waged by this organization to preserve the Spanish language in Puerto Rico is proof of this.

This nomination brings me back to the people that made possible my development as a Puerto Rican writer: first of all to my mother, Lorencita Ramírez de Arellano, who graduated from UPR in 1926 with a double major in education and Spanish. She awakened in me the love of Spanish literature, and it was in her book lined with notes that I read the *Arcipreste de Hita* for the first time. I also want to thank

Margot Arce de Vázquez; Manuel Porras Cruz; Pablo García Díaz; Enrique Laguerre; Luis Arrigoitía; José Ramón de la Torre; Federico Acevedo, my MA thesis director; Arcadio Díaz Quiñones; Francisco Manrique Cabrera; Ángel Rama; Mario Vargas Llosa; and other professors at the University of Puerto Rico who were my teachers and gave me inspiration. And my deepest gratitude to my husband, the architect Agustín Costa, for his unconditional support and generous care during the writing of the marathon that was *La casa de la laguna*, and of many other texts. And I want to thank Professor Julio Ortega, who has been my Virgil, the wise master and generous mentor of my literary career, and of that of many other Puerto Rican writers. Finally, my heartfelt gratitude goes to Luce López-Baralt for her support and true friendship of many years, dating back to the time when we were fellow students in Mario Vargas Llosa's classes at UPR.

I would like to point out that the generation of Puerto Rican writers to which I belong, the Generation of 1970, helped to keep our Spanish tongue alive. Our generation of Puerto Rican writers was the first to experiment with literary language in a way that was dramatic and shocking—a fact that has yet to be studied. Back then, and from different places—among them the pages of the journal *Zona. Carga y descarga*—we threw ourselves into the open sea of writing; bare-chested, we broke the rules and mental structures, we did violence to our spelling and syntax, we incorporated into literature the supposedly vile language of the streets, we invented neologisms according to the demands and circumstances of the time, and in the end we assimilated all the variegated vocabulary that our technical, scientific, and multicultural world requires today. Umberto Eco had proclaimed "the open work," and we tried to invent a language without beginning or end, without punctuation marks or social distinctions, without an upper or lower case. The first editorial of *Zona* had unmistakable surrealist echoes; it read:

You can always come in and out of *Zona* freely, zone of bodies
with holes, zoneofillusion, zoneofsound, notsosacredzone like
a new game played without rules jack be nimble jack be quick
(load), jack jumped over the candlestick (unload). We condemn
the pompous journals loaded with entablatures, cornices, ionic-
doriccorinthian editorial columns, with sin-taxis, we skate in the
galleries of logic and scholarship because their flagstones are fun
and we oil our ball bearings so that the clickety clickety clack
itstoolate itstoolate itstoolate of the sidewalk disappears and our
chattering teeth travel silently and smoothly to eternity.[2]

The rebellion of the writers of the 1970s had a lot to do with the
world-wide struggle for civil rights that began in 1968. In Paris and
Mexico City students marched together with workers for liberty and
for a better world. In 1972, the first volume of the journal *Zona. Carga
y descarga* was published; it included many writers and artists of the
1970s, like Manuel Ramos Otero, Luis César Rivera, Francis Shwartz,
Tomás López Ramírez, Zilia Sánchez, Luis López Nieves, Juan
Antonio Ramos, Etna Iris Rivera, Iván Sillén, Edgardo Rodríguez
Juliá, Olga Nolla, Vanessa Droz, Ivonne Ochart, and many others.
In *Zona 5* (1973), Luis Rafael Sánchez published a chapter of *La
guaracha del Macho Camacho* (1976), a work that was at the center of
the renovation of Puerto Rican literature. Luis Rafael became the
most prominent figure of the Generation of 1970 because of his
revolutionary use of language.

Puerto Rican writers before our generation were known for
the immaculate correctness of their literary language. From Manuel
Alonso to José Luis González, including the works of Enrique Laguerre,
Tomás Blanco, Antonio S. Pedreira, René Marqués, Pedro Juan Soto,
and Emilio Díaz Valcárcel, among many others, Puerto Rican writers
struggled with a classical, elegant, cultured Spanish so as to put their
Hispanic identity beyond any doubt. They respected grammatical
norms and followed the rules of linguistic decorum as was proper
to intellectuals who belonged to the great family of Latin American
culture, which was made up of many different people. To write and
speak Spanish correctly was part of our conscientious pride; it was a
statement of our dignity in spite of our difficult political situation.

The rebellion and rupture of the generation of 1970 changed all of that. Our rebellion was against the Mother, not against the Father; it was against the mother tongue that had protected Puerto Rican writers for so long. The writers of the 1970s rebelled against the classical norms that were drying up the soul of our literature. More play was needed, more freedom of space. Anarchy-prone writers like Iván Sillén and Juan Ramón Meléndez (*El Che*), Voltairean free thinkers like Edgardo Rodríguez Juliá, and feminists like Liliana Ramos, Olga Nolla, and Ana Lydia Vega were all a part of a new way of thinking that opposed all order and all dogma. We were familiar with the works of the Surrealists from our classes with Ángel Rama, and there was an important precedent for this in Puerto Rico: the lessons of the Republican refugees from the Spanish Civil War, which taught us to give value to our vision. We have yet to study and truly understand the significance and the effect of the presence and creativity of figures like Francisco Vázquez (Compostela), Cristóbal Ruiz, José Vela Zanetti, Ángel Botello Barros, Pedro Salinas, and Juan Ramón Jiménez and others, on our Island.

In *Zona. Carga y descarga* we cultivated a space for freedom that was highly criticized for its lack of commitment to a Marxist and socialist vision. The left called us elitists living in an ivory tower, and the right accused us of being radical, intellectual terrorists. It was true that *Zona* tried to accomplish something completely different from other journals that were nevertheless essential, such as *Asomante* (later *Sin nombre*) as well as *Guajana* and *Ventana*. We worked within the general framework of political independence, but we did not subscribe to any particular ideology, and I think we never felt comfortable in any political party. We protested against what appeared to us a stagnant society, against a past that we had to overcome by breaking the traditional boundaries of society, of politics, of the Church, of literature, and of highbrow culture. The gradual importance of the literature written after the sixties by Puerto Ricans living in exile also led us to accept a literary language that was less "pure," and more open to experimentation than before. The increased use of English after 1970 in our vernacular, the mixing of both languages into a contradictory Spanglish, was both enriching and regrettable, and was another reality we could not escape. The language of a people is in a constant state of transformation, and, to quote from the *Diálogo* by Juan de Valdés (written in 1530), "I write as I speak," or language follows usage, and not the other way around.

The rupture and the renovation of language has been the guiding principle of my journey as a writer. Even when I published *La casa de la laguna* (*The House on the Lagoon*) in 1995, my first book published in English (there is a first version of this book which I wrote in Spanish but which never saw the light of day), my intention was always, first and foremost, to reach a wider audience, and secondly, to awaken language from the stupor of perfection where it rested. I believe that rebellion is the most important value when fundamentalism and terrorism are the order of the day, whether it is a life led according to existentialist principles, or according to anarchy and based on aesthetic principles.

I feel that two different literary traditions and two different languages "duel" or confront one another in my work and within me. I never gave way to Spanglish in my work; instead I incorporated different aspects of English into the main stream of Puerto Rican literature. It was like seeing the world through a different lens, one that broadened the meaning of life. I tried to convey this idea in my poem "Corriente alterna/Alternating current," published in the book *Duelo del lenguaje/Language Duel*. "English is an aerodynamic language / Thoughts fire away in it / like lightning strikes... Our tongue is very different. / It is humid and profound / with so many curves and circuitous paths that make us feel like / astronauts of the uterus..." But there is another meaning of the word "duelo" that is important in that book. The "duelo" of the title is ambiguous and also refers to a dirge, sung for the Spanish of our beloved Lope de Vega and Cervantes, for the unrecoverable loss of their classical world. This loss hurts me deeply. But on the other hand, there have always been key moments when literature in Spanish has renewed itself in a dialogue with other languages: with Italian, as was the case of the poet Garcilaso de la Vega; with French, in the case of Rubén Darío; with English, in the case of Borges. In Puerto Rico this dialogue has been with popular languages that are alive, creative, and critical, and the

young with their new technologies of communication have turned Spanish into a new popular language.

My nomination as an honorary member of the Puerto Rican Academy of the Spanish Language fills me with joy because it validates my core values and those I have lived as a writer. It recognizes the value of rebellion and its importance today, when dangerous fundamentalist tendencies of all types are gaining strength. I am honored by this nomination because it gives value to my work with language, and it recognizes the influence of a generation of which I am proud to be a part.

NOTES

1. The essay was written on the occasion of Rosario Ferré's induction as an honorary member of the Puerto Rican Academy of the Spanish Language, December 19, 2007, in the Ballajá Barracks, Old San Juan. Luce López-Baralt read the essay on Rosario Ferré's behalf.

2. This avant-garde manifesto originally appeared in the first number of *Zona. Carga y descarga*. The Spanish original reads as follows: "De *Zona* se puede siempre entrar y salir libremente, zona cuerpo de huecos, sonailusión, sonasonora, sonanó sagrada como un juego nuevo que se juega sin leyes brinca la tablita yo ya la brinqué (carga), bríncala tú ahora que yo me cansé (descarga). Denunciamos la pomposidad de las revistas cargadas de cornisas, entabladuras, editoriales columnas jonicasdoricascorintias, sin taxis, corremos patines por las galerías de la lógica y de la escolástica porque tienen unas losas grandes que son chéveres y aceitamos los bolines y desaparece el yapaqué yapaqué yapaqué de las aceras y los dientes se deslizan silenciosos y tranquilos hacia la eternidad" (translator's note).